Write Naked!

Secrets of Dynamic Prose Laid Bare

Josh Langston

Also by Josh Langston

~Janda Books~
Novels:
Treason, Treason!
Resurrection Blues
A Little Primitive
A Little More Primitive
A Primitive in Paradise
Under Saint Owain's Rock

Short story collections:
Mysfits
Six From Greeley
Dancing Among the Stars
Christmas Beyond the Box
Who Put Scoundrels in Charge?

~Edge Science Fiction and Fantasy Publishing~
Druids
Captives
Warriors

(** with Barbara Galler-Smith)

DEDICATION

This book is dedicated to Annel Martin, an astonishing woman who has been an inspiration to me since the day we met. She showed up in the first writing class I ever taught, soaked up everything I had to offer, and wanted more. Over time we developed a friendship that I treasure. Her perseverance in the face of too many obstacles--my writing instruction being but a minor one--has proven her to be a woman of immense character and great fortitude. I look forward to modeling one of my heroines after her.

I must also give a nod to all the other eager learners who suffered through my writing classes while I figured out how to teach this bizarre but rewarding craft. I realize now that art cannot be taught. The best one can hope to impart is an appreciation for tools and techniques.

This book contains a great deal of material which I learned through trial and error, mostly error. I'd like to think I can save new writers a little time and a lot of grief by sharing the stuff that works. That's my intention, anyway.

Good luck to all who give it a try!

~*~

CONTENTS

ACKNOWLEDGMENTS

In grateful recognition of my First Readers and fellow verb mongers:
Doris Reidy, Pam Olinto, Doug Davis, Amy Hunkler,
Faye Martin, V. Masters, and Robin Castillo.
Without their invaluable assistance,
this work would not have been
possible, let alone likely.

Thanks, guys!

Introduction
Write Naked?

Write in the buff? Nonsense. So why the bizarre title? Because *just* writing isn't enough. Pumping out a few words, or even a few hundred *thousand*, doesn't make someone a writer--at least, not in my vocabulary.

Writers should communicate on multiple levels. A writer must be willing to make the effort to reach readers in a variety of ways. Have you done enough to insure that your readers can easily visualize a scene? Does it intrigue? Does the dialog feel real? Would your reader want to grab a bite to eat with your protagonist, or see your villain get twenty to life? Do readers share the emotions of your characters? Was the book hard to put down? Did your readers hate knowing the story would end soon?

Getting positive answers to these questions means you must put everything you have into the work. Dig to find the right word, the best phrase, the most meaningful description. In 1960's parlance, if you want to succeed, you need to let it all hang out. *ALL of it!* That's what writing naked means to me. Fortunately, learning how doesn't have to be boring. You're allowed to laugh along the way!

~*~

How to Read this Book
Or Maybe, Just Why.

Surely no one in this day and age needs to be told how to read a book. You just open it and dive in. Right? Well....

This is, above all else, a textbook. It purports to teach certain skills about the craft of fiction writing. But there's more to it than that. It can also teach non-writers a little bit about what goes *into* good writing. What makes a story compelling, for instance. Why are some books so damned hard to put down, late at night, when you know you have to get up early and do the 9-to-5 thing?

But this isn't *just* a textbook. It's also a humor book. It's meant to cause readers to smile, maybe even giggle--right out loud! If good fiction should both inform and entertain, why can't those same goals apply to non-fiction? There's no law that says instruction can't be fun. I admit it may not be entirely appropriate in certain circumstances, like executioner training, but more often than not, folks learn just as well, if not better, when they're smiling.

So, read on. Be happy, and learn!

~*~

Chapter 1
A Formula for Fiction?

I had been writing fiction for several years before I had the chance to attend a workshop presented by Kris Rusch and Dean Wesley Smith. This husband and wife team has achieved near legendary status in the speculative fiction writing world. They have both produced a prodigious volume of high quality fiction across several genres and under a variety of names. Fortunately for me, in addition to their professional editing and publishing efforts, they found time to lead workshops for writers at all levels of achievement. I didn't get much sleep that weekend, but I sure learned a lot.

Fiction Formula

Arguably the most valuable instruction I received was on something called **7-Point Plotting**. It was originally devised by Algys Budrys, another legend among speculative fiction writers. I have used it ever since and offer it to anyone interested in producing well-rounded stories.

Every story should have a beginning, a middle and an end. That's easy enough.

Budrys, known to his friends as "AJ," broke this down further. He postulated that a good Opening (the beginning) consisted of three distinct elements: Character, Setting, and Conflict.

I find it easier to summarize these as: **a Person, in a Place, with a Problem.**

> **A Good Opening Will Feature:**
> **A Person,**
> **In a Place,**
> **With a Problem.**

1. **Person** -- Usually, but not always, the primary character in the story. People work best, although there's no law against starring an animal, an alien, or an Apricot. Most folks like reading about... folks.

2. **Place** -- Where does the action take place? In a courtroom? A spaceship? In Captain Kangaroo's basement? An interesting setting will often grab a reader when the conflict is weak.

3. **Problem** -- This could be the primary focus of the tale, or it could be a lesser issue. But every opening must have an element of Conflict, because <u>that's</u> what grabs a reader.

Next comes the **Middle,** and according to Budrys, this consists of one or more <u>paired</u> concepts:

4. **Try** -- This is the effort usually made by the protagonist to resolve the main Problem of the story. Each such effort is paired with item 5: a Fail.

5. **Fail** -- Not all fails are fails! Sometimes a protagonist will succeed, only to find that the original problem has gotten worse. As expected, failure will lead to

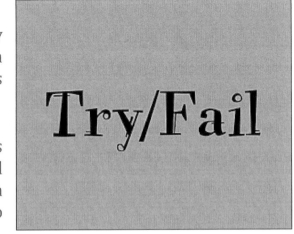

more difficulty, too. Most short stories use one or two Try/Fail sequences. Novels often go through dozens.

At some point, the story will reach the **End**. Budrys broke this down, too.

6. **Climax** -- This is the result of the final Try/Fail, the most dramatic and far-reaching. Success or failure here could mean life or death for the protagonist. It is the culmination of all the efforts of all the characters to force a solution to the Problem.

7. **Denouement** -- This is what Mark Twain called the "Marryin' and the Buryin'," and that's a very succinct way to describe it. It amounts to a summary of who survived the Climax.

The point of all this is NOT to suggest that you should address each of these elements specifically while working. I've found the most effective way to use the scheme is to wait until you've finished a story. If it works, and you're happy with it, move on. If it doesn't work, then break out the 7-Point chart and see if there's something missing.

This illustrates the 7 Points as they are fully incorporated.

The main goal of this method is to provide writers with a way to ensure that he or she

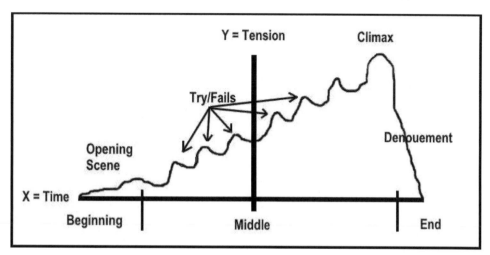

has at least considered everything important in a typical speculative fiction story. That said, many famous and successful stories have been written which minimize or even ignore a point or two. Such stories are usually written by masters of the craft, folks who have labored in the field for what often seems like an eternity. They deserve to be able to take short cuts. Lesser writers do so at their own risk.

Try this for practice:

Write a story opening--*right now!* Create a character, put him or her in a recognizable place, and give them a problem. Do it in three paragraphs or less.

Here's an example:

One of the wheels on Harry's grocery cart wasn't completely round. It thumped constantly and in cadence with his headache. Somehow he managed to find everything on the list his wife had crammed into his wallet along with the admonition that the evening meal was a life or death proposition. Who didn't love dinner with his mother-in-law?

Harry pushed the heavily laden cart to the check-out counter and unloaded it. That's when he discovered his wallet was missing.

~*~

Chapter 2
In the Beginning

Having finished ten novels, I have a pretty clear idea how it's done. And, with the exception of my first effort, which now resides in a landfill somewhere, I fully believe the books I've written are worth reading. Those with an historical element might even be instructive, though that's never been my *raison d'être*.

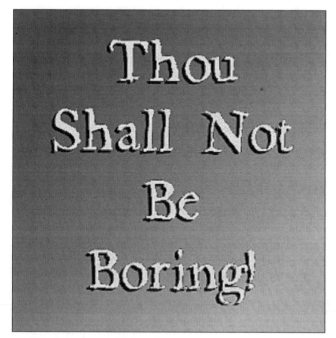

My primary goal has always been to entertain.

If what I write doesn't hold a reader's interest, what's the point? "Watch me pile up facts" is no way to win hearts and influence minds. And I've gotta do both. I want *every* reader to tell someone else how much they like my work. This will generate more readers, more endorsements, and at some point, better living conditions. (Full disclosure: I want a cozy little retirement castle on a white sand beach that I can pay for with never-ending royalties.)

9

Okay, I'm not that much of an optimist, but it would sure be nice to have a place that wouldn't wash away when the tide comes in. That's not too much to ask, is it?

So, how does one write something entertaining? If you're a human being with a modest understanding of logic and a fundamental grasp of the language, you have the skills to do it. (You'll also need the ability to keep working until it's done, but that's a subject for another chapter.)

Pssst: here's the secret:

Step One: Create a character with a _Strong motive_; make him *Do something* about it, and then hit him with the *consequences*.

Step Two: Create another character with a _conflicting_ motive. Now, make *her _do something_* about it. When you're done, hit her with the *consequences* of _her_ action.

On examination, the two steps are nearly identical. The big difference is the word **conflicting** in step two. That difference is crucial, as are the requirements for motive, action, and consequences.

Think about your favorite stories. In most cases there's a character you like, and another one you don't: Peter Pan and Captain Hook, Ahab and the whale, the Green Bay Packers and the Dallas Cowboys. Whatever. They have goals which they try to achieve despite facing someone with a different outcome in mind to which they are fully committed.

It's a model that has worked--and will continue to work--forever. Cave-dwelling storytellers wove tales of heroes and villains, monsters and men, good gods and bad gods. And they didn't even have a written language, so you're already WAY ahead of them!

Once you know who you're writing about, get busy. **Remember:** you *don't* have to write the whole book in one sitting. Nobody does that. You only have to work on one small part of the story: a scene. Just one. Could be big or small. Doesn't matter. What does matter is that it must focus on one of the elements mentioned above (motive, action, consequence). **Then:** don't start scene two until you've finished scene one.

I know writers who don't write their scenes in order. They might do the first action scene, then the climax, then a love scene, then God only knows what. When they're all done, they "assemble" the scenes in a finished order. I can't imagine doing that. At least, not without a highly detailed outline. Assuming you're working on your first book, I suggest you try a less gymnastic approach: write 'em in order. Revise and rearrange as needed. Add new stuff later.

For me, sequential order works best. I write the motivational scene for character one, then the same for character two. After that I write the action for character one, and the same for character two. Ditto for consequences. At this point, the two players may have already beaten each other into pulpy little piles. So I write a scene in which one or both of them heal, and in the process stumble onto yet another motive. *Et voilà!* The cycle repeats.

Okay, that's a vastly simplified approach, but it's the heart of the process. Neil Gaiman is quoted as saying, "This is how you do it; you sit down at the keyboard and you put one word after another until it's done. It's that easy, and that hard."

Try this for practice:

Dream up two characters--male/female, boss/worker, whatever. Give them motivations that clash.

Here's an example:

Black Bart hadn't eaten in two days. The can of beans he stole from a murdered prospector barely kept him alive. Only a supreme strength of will allowed him to focus on the bank in Plattville. The payroll for the railroad would be stored there, and he wanted it. He needed it. He by-gawd *deserved* it.

Lowell Luvheart had been the sheriff of Doober county for all of 24 hours. The mayor's daughter had a lot to do with that. She'd convinced her daddy that no one was more capable of protecting the citizens of Plattville, or their property, than Lowell, and Lowell aimed to prove her right. Now if he could just find someone to sell him a gun and maybe show him how to shoot it, he'd be just fine.

~*~

Chapter 3
Putting Meat on the Bones

Okay, you've got an opening done, and it's pretty spiffy. Now what? Is this where the Try/Fail thingy comes in? How does that work?

Watch carefully now. See? There's nothing up my sleeves....

Let's say you've got a character in mind. We'll call him Al. Fair 'nuff? This is just for practice, so you can change name, sex, race, religion, hair color, number of teeth--*whatever*--later.

So, what drives old Al? What's his passion in life? What is it that keeps him awake nights? Just for the hell of it, let's say his goal in life **is** to sleep well at night. Seems reasonable. (Make a note to come back to that at the very end of whatever tale we manage to create.)

Now, <u>what's standing in the way</u>? A neighbor's dog? A nearby airport? World hunger? We need to pick something and roll with it. For now, just play along with me, okay? Let's say it's the neighbor's dog, because, well, why not? Besides, I <u>love</u> dogs.

13

Okay, Al can't sleep because of the neighbor's mutt. Not very sexy, is it? Let's spice it up a tad. We'll make Al's real name Algonquin. He hates it, of course, and the only thing keeping him from making a legal name change is a shortage of cash. He'd rather spend what little he earns--from his job as a junk sorter in a recycling plant--on life's essentials, plus a lottery ticket or two. Nah, make that three. Apparently, Al is also short on self-discipline.

And his neighbor, Zenobia, a part-time lingerie model and occasional car show hostess, can't seem to remember to feed her 105-lb. Rottweiler, "Precious." Either that, or she's off working, and there's no one left at home to take care of it.

Al considers various remedies for getting the dog to shut up. These might include shooting, drugging, kidnapping, or possibly just duct taping the critter's jaws together. They do it to alligators on TV all the time, so why not?

Think for a moment, however. Each of those four options provides an opportunity for action--Al can *try* to do something to solve his problem. In a bad

story, the first thing he attempts will work. But we don't want to write a bad story. I don't, anyway! And, since I'm driving this thing, I'm going to insist that Al attempt, or at least seriously consider, trying three of these four options.

Further, for each attempt, good ol' Al must fall short of his goal. Maybe he can't find a gun, or if he does, he lives in an area where discharging a firearm without due cause is against the law, and the guy living on the *other* side of Zenobia's house is a cop or a district attorney (who must be hard of hearing).

Drugging seems an easy task, but stealing pills from someone who needs them is beneath Al, and he doesn't have a prescription for anything suitable. He could scrounge around on the seedy side of town, hoping to score something, but he's clearly not "cool" enough to get away with it. Any self-respecting drug dealer would find him suspicious in the extreme. So, nope, that won't work either.

Kidnapping? A 105-pound Rottweiler? Which barks, all darn night? Yeah, sure. Forget kidnapping little Precious. And if kidnapping is out of the question, taping the monster's jaws together isn't much of an option either, assuming Al would prefer to keep his appendages intact.

Well, just damn! What'll we do now?

We'll simply have ol' Al walk next door and confront Zenobia. When he does, however, he falls under her spell--those amazingly amber, soul-eating eyes of

hers put him completely off his game. He stutters, coughs, and dissembles and never quite manages to ask her to keep her dadgum dog in the house at night. Instead, he falls in love.

Which is when Zenobia's phone rings. From the half of the conversation he can hear, Al deduces that his heartthrob's booking agent is on the line, and he wants her to report for work at an underworld car show, only instead of wearing her usual car show costume--a short skirt and tight top--he wants her in what she wears for her modeling gigs: racy underwear.

Zenobia says she's not that kinda gal, and she has no desire to associate with the mob types who will be attending the show. Her agent gives her an ultimatum and hangs up.

And suddenly, we have a story in the making. Will it become a novel? Could be. That all depends on where we decide to take it.

But wait! What if we've got this all wrong, not only about the pooch, but about the sweet young thing next door, too?

What if Zenobia has an entirely different agenda? Maybe her whole aim is to get close to that mob boss either because she's secretly working for a competitor, or because she's really some sort of undercover (well, barely-covered) cop?

Or, if neither of those options work, there's always the chance she could… I think you get the picture. The whole Try/Fail thing is predicated on the efforts a character makes to change the status quo.

In the first chapter we discussed 7-Point Plotting. In the second chapter we took a look at the machinery of fiction: Motive, Action, and Consequence. Thus far we've featured the Motive and Action elements, but we haven't really covered the issue of Consequence, and it's just as important as the others.

Consequence can be broken down into four critical parts. [Don't panic! This will be easier than you think. Just bear with me (and Jim Butcher, the **New York Times** bestselling novelist who first blogged about it).] If you want to develop character-driven fiction that readers just can't put down, you'd be well advised to cover each of these points--in the order prescribed here. They are:

- ❖ An **emotional reaction** to what just happened, followed by
- ❖ A **review and evaluation** of what just happened, followed by
- ❖ The **anticipation** of a response to what just happened, followed by
- ❖ A **choice** based on the foregoing.

That may sound like a lot of stuff, and it is, at least in terms of importance. The order is also critically important, because that's precisely the way we crazy human beings react to just about every consequential event.

Think back to the last fender-bender you experienced. (Those of you who haven't been through one will just have to be creative; try substituting some other calamity.) Okay, ready?

Honk! Squeal! Crunch!

1) Your initial reaction is purely **emotional**, and questions race through your brain: what happened? Who's responsible? Was anyone hurt? Will I be arrested?

2) Next, you'll mentally **replay** what just happened, and you'll try to **evaluate** your situation and answer some or all of the questions you just asked yourself.

3) Once you've got a handle on what happened, you'll immediately start working on how you'll respond. Maybe you've been drinking, and the cops are coming, and you'd better sneak off into the woods. OR, maybe you've had some first aid training, and you know someone's hurt, and they need you. OR maybe you're the one who's hurt, and YOU need help, and you'd better DO something! In other words, you **anticipate** what to do next.

4) Finally, you make a **choice** about what to do, and this translates into the next Try/Fail episode.

Neat, huh? You've come full circle through the Try/Fail cycle. Now, depending on the genre you're writing for--and if you're not sure, hang on until we get through chapter 5--you can give the various steps a wide variety of attention. Romance stories will obviously focus more on emotion and anticipation. Mysteries and Science Fiction will delve deeper into logical issues about what happened and why. Westerns, fantasies, thrillers, cozies, and all the rest will emphasize those items which appeal the most to those audiences.

The great advantage of all this, and the reason you need to do it, is simply this: it ties your reader to your character **psychologically**. Your reader will know and understand why your character does something, even if they completely disagree with what the character chooses to do. And, they'll want more.

So, I urge you--***right now!***--to grab a sticky note and jot down the following:

- ❖ **Try/Fail**
    - o **Motivation**
    - o **Action**
    - o **Consequence**
        - ▪ **Emotional response**
        - ▪ **Replay and evaluation**
        - ▪ **Anticipation**
        - ▪ **Choice**
- ❖ **Rinse and repeat**

Now, paste that note somewhere on your monitor where you'll see it when you're working on your next masterpiece.

Try this for practice:

Pick a character of your own and devise both a goal and an obstacle. Imagine an outcome and then diagnose the consequences.

Here's an example:

You're kidding, right? This whole chapter is an example! Time to cowboy up (Sorry ladies. You may cow*girl* up) and write something. A couple big, fat paragraphs oughta do it. Get crackin'.

~*~

Chapter 4
Who You Lookin' At?

Before I go sailing off on another tangent I need to talk about a topic that's often overlooked, but it's something quite a few of my writing students have asked me about. It's called point of view. Or, more interestingly, point of view *shifting*.

POV shifts are not a big deal and generally aren't too hard to fix, but folks new to the craft need to be aware of them. In most of the popular fiction produced these days, writers use either first or third person limited viewpoint.

SageOfTheSouth.wordpress.com

First person, of course, is "I." Third person is "he," "she," or "it." So in a first person story, everything the reader learns is filtered through the character known as "I" or "me." As in: *I* saw this, or *I* tasted that, or *I* grew tired and took a nap. Everything happens to *me!*

19

From the drink's perspective, the martini had her.

SageOfTheSouth.wordpress.com

In third person, everything is experienced via someone else. Suzie saw this, or tasted that, or she got thirsty and had a honkin' big martini (with cantaloupe-size olives). *You go, girl!*

Sorry.

The word "limited" in the viewpoint description is the important one. It describes the number of potential heads the writer intends to use--per scene--to convey information. There are only two options: <u>one</u> ("limited"), and <u>more than one</u> ("omniscient"). The writer will either stay in one wad of gray matter, or he's decided to wander through the world, popping willy-nilly into any (and potentially "every") such wad he encounters.

Here's an example of limited viewpoint. Everything readers learn is filtered through a single character:

Young Jamie stumbled into a dark alley to relieve himself. He'd just been told his girlfriend had dumped him. He reached the back of the alley, but before he could unburden himself, he heard a noise from the street and turned to see what it was. Silhouetted against a streetlamp, stood a huge man. Jamie tried to swallow, but all the fluids in his body had collected in his bladder. When the brute began to run toward him, Jamie's bladder gave way. He dug in his pocket to retrieve the off-brand stun gun he'd bought for protection. He aimed it at the approaching hulk and pressed the button.

Now, let's try this same scene without restricting the viewpoint. I'll mark the shifts by underlining the darker character's input.

Jamie stood at the back of the alley, fumbling with his zipper, when he heard a noise from the street. He turned to look. <u>Biff strained to see into the darkness at the end of the alley. He knew he'd seen someone scuttle back there. This was Biff's alley, by Gawd. Nobody messed around in there without his permission. He had to investigate. And fast!</u> Jamie tried to swallow, but his throat had gone dry. The brute at

the end of the alley was coming toward him at a gallop. Jamie ignored his zipper; it was too late for that anyway, and concentrated on extracting his discount store stun gun from his pocket. <u>As Biff's eyes adjusted to the dark, he could see a scrawny punk pulling something from his pants pocket. A gun? *Probably*. Biff raced forward, hoping to take the runt by surprise.</u> Jamie pressed the button on the stun thingie, hoping he had it aimed in the right direction. It made a tiny fizzy sound, and an instant later, a man-shaped building landed on top of him.

The second scenario might actually work if the POV shifts were given separate micro-scenes with a suitable visual device--either an extra blank line or some sort of marker (I like flying splats: ~*~). If left lumped together, however, there's just too much back and forth. Keep that up for page after page and your reader will feel like they've been watching a ping pong match from one end of the net. Whiplash, anyone?

Do yourself, and your readers, a huge favor. Stick to one point of view per scene. There are probably a dozen reasons for not following this advice, the biggest being what to do when your point of view character dies. Somebody's got to pick up the slack, right? So, I'll give you a free pass on those. But the others?

Nope. Play by the rules!

Try this for practice:

Assuming you might still be just a little rusty when it comes to shifting points of view, I've included a little exercise for you in the **Appendix**, and it's not even very hard. It is, however, worth a giggle or two. So, go give the **Point of View Challenge** a try.

~*~

Chapter 5
Don't Need No Stinkin' Genre

We left off earlier with a "what if" after sketching a quick look at a couple primary characters in a contemporary, non-fantasy setting. (Okay, the lingerie model issue may have been a bit of fantasy.) Point is, one of the MANY things I *didn't* discuss is genre. What if you don't care to write a modern action/adventure story? Maybe your preferred field is science fiction, or romance, or mystery, or high fantasy, or any of the umpty dozen other varieties of fiction (except minimalist {cringe}, we don't talk about *that* kinda writing around here).

Could Al and Zenobia be manipulated enough to fit some of those other molds? Probably. And without a great deal of difficulty. Let's try it. Take a look at these alternative takes on the characters and story line presented in the previous chapter. Be prepared to use at least a little imagination to make these work.

Science Fiction -- Start by making one of the primary characters an alien. I'm including the dog in that group. (Robert Heinlein, one of my favorite authors, did a great YA novel about a kid who adopted an alien critter as a pet.)

Western -- The dog is tied up outside a neighboring trailer among wranglers on a rodeo circuit, or a neighboring wagon on the Oregon Trail, or a double-wide on the outskirts of Tumbleweed, Texas.

Romance -- Wait. Al's already fallen for Zenobia. Now we just have to make them pine for each other despite muddied motives and encounters with false loves. Or is that *historical* fiction? Sometimes I get confused.

Mystery -- Someone poisoned the dog. But who did it and why? What other crime(s) might they be covering up?

High fantasy -- Zenobia's agent is an evil wizard, and Al is a down-on-his-luck knight who still can't sleep.

Military/Spy/Thriller -- The dog belongs to the ambassador of a European ally, and he's wearing an explosive collar.

My point is that no matter where you intend to peddle your masterpiece, building it requires that you start *somewhere*. You can tailor the details as needed to fit a genre with which you're comfortable. For me, contemporary action/adventure is where it's at, but our discussion should apply equally well to any form of popular fiction.

What we're talking about boils down to two closely related essentials: **Conflict** and **Complication**. Good novels have it, bad novels don't. And mediocre novels probably don't have enough.

[Full disclosure: I'm a genre fiction snob; I admit it. Reading about teen angst, probing the unconscious for signs of self-worth, contemplating the power of introspection or fostering a deep seated need to feel guilty are pursuits--God willing--you'll never find in my work.]

If there's no conflict, there's no story; adding complication is the easiest way to provide conflict.

So, it's not enough for Al to simply be in love, nor is it enough for Zenobia to be in jeopardy. Those two things might serve nicely to get the ball rolling, but once it's moving, you've got to provide some bumps in the road, or maybe a massive sinkhole or a washed out bridge, or-- Get the idea? Make trouble for your players. It doesn't matter if the problems are big or small, but keep 'em coming.

If you choose to tell Al's story from Al's point of view, and Zenobia's story from Zenobia's point of view, you can switch back and forth whenever things become perilous. Al races to the auto show, but the road is slick from a recent rain, and his brakes aren't all that great anyway, so when a fawn trundles out of the woods in front of him he tries to stop but only manages to spin wildly in the road. Suddenly, a gigantic oak tree appears from nowhere.

[Blink--scene break--Time to get into Zenobia's head....]

25

Zenobia's agent, Slim Bagadirt, introduces her to a high-ranking partner in a

local waste management business who has a proposition for her. He pats his knee, a la Santa Claus, and offers her a seat. After all, he looks sorta like her uncle Bert. She settles in and listens. All she has to do is--

[*Blink*--scene break--Back to Al....]

The car hits the tree instead of the sweet little Bambi clone. Fortunately, the collision takes out the back half of the vehicle rather than either half of Al. He stumbles away from the wreck, shaken but alive. Still woozy, he steps into the road hoping to thumb a ride when he hears the unmistakable blare of an 18-wheeler's air horn. He turns and--

[*Blink*--scene break--Zenobia...]

Outraged by the mobster's proposal, Zenobia leaps up from his lap, slaps him in the face, and bolts toward the

exit. There she encounters a man roughly the size of a California redwood who grabs her and escorts her to a waiting van. She protests, but--

[*Blink*--scene break--Etc.]

I like to have several point of view characters available. This allows me more leeway in thinking up nasty problems for them. I've found it very helpful to maintain a simple chart listing the scenes in order by point of view character. In addition I include a line of text to describe the action. It's also a handy place to make notes about character names, personal details, and anything else I'm likely to forget. (More on that later.)

Try this for practice:

Write a paragraph or two focusing on a character with a problem in a setting of your choice. Then rewrite the paragraph to put the same character with essentially the same problem in a completely different genre, perhaps in a different era. Then do it again with yet another genre in mind.

You might even want to experiment changing your character's gender, but leaving everything else the same.

(If you think you're up to it, there's an additional exercise in the **Appendix** which will test your ability to work in various genres. Go check out the **Time and Place Challenge**.)

~*~

Chapter 6
Don't Begin at the Beginning

I blame biographies. And "education." As school kids in America, we aren't allowed to read about Abraham Lincoln, the 16th president of the United States, unless we first read through umpteen tedious chapters recounting in excruciating detail his upbringing in a log cabin in Illinois, or Kentucky, or some godforsaken place in Indianastan.

If you grew up in the UK, you probably learned all about Winston Churchill's connection to the House of Marlborough before you read anything about him extracting Britain's collective chestnuts from the blitz-fed bonfires of World War Two.

Why is that? Because there's damned little taught about writing fiction in school! "Educators" have no time for it, and because *they* learned everything they know in linear fashion, then by Gawd so will every little Bobby, Sue and Malik who wanders into the building. Thus we come to equate studying by candlelight with emancipating slaves--at least as far as storytelling goes.

Which, for fiction writers, is just plain dumb!

The "beginning" doesn't refer to the happy collision of sperm and egg which led to the hero's conception. The "beginning" happens at the exact moment where bad shit overcomes everything else; where *status quo* becomes *status crunch*; where the rubber meets the rabbit on the road, or where the hero loses his horse, his house, and his grip on reality.

Technically, it's called *in media res*, which is fancy schmancy Latin for "Holy crap!" (Or, for you scholars out there, "in the middle of things," which may be more accurate, but is way less fun.)

What puzzles me, is why so many beginning writers *don't* get it. 'Cause the great hulking majority of readers have no trouble with it at all. They've already learned all they want to know about Abe's humble origins. They weren't wild about it in school, and they sure as hell don't care about it now. They want to see the Ol' Rail Splitter being chased by the vampire he intended to skewer with

a two-foot long wooden kabob. In-Media-Freakin'-Res, baby! It wasn't always this way. There was a time, somewhere in the 19th century probably, when we didn't think of everything in terms of sound bites, MTV, and/or elevator pitches. These things, among others, have bludgeoned us into demanding double shots of espresso laden action from the get go. It ain't fair, and it ain't normal, but it's the way it is. If you want to write popular fiction, you've gotta follow the popfic "rules" or whatever it is that passes for 'em.

Once you've proven your mastery of the form, and built an audience willing to forgive you, and

29

deposited your first gazillion bucks in royalties, you can start your stories anyway you please. Or, if you're too impatient for that, you can just self-publish. All those big name 19th century writers did it. You can, too. For now, however, you've got to snag the reader's attention, and you'd best do it in the first paragraph. The first sentence of the first paragraph would be nice, but we haven't gone that far off the deep end, yet. What you don't want to do is haul in a dump truck load of background material and deposit it at ground zero.

It may seem logical to explain little Filbert's fascination with small breed wild dogs *before* he wanders off into the woods with a pack of pygmy werewolves, but experience has shown--over and over again--that readers prefer to skip the history and jump into the action. They don't have to know why it's logical just now. If you make it real, and make Filbert sympathetic, readers will be perfectly happy.

Try this for practice:

Write a story opening in which your point of view character faces a life and death situation *in the first sentence*. Make it dramatic. Make your readers squirm. Indeed, make *yourself* squirm!

~*~

Chapter 7
Whut's That Ya Say?

Good dialog isn't real, it just *feels* that way. Say *what?* Oy. There goes Langston, on his way 'round the bend. Again. But seriously, just listen to the "normal" conversation below and you'll understand:

"Hey, Joe!"
"Dude! How's it goin'?"
"Not bad, not bad, And you?"
"Okay. Same old, same old, y'know?"
"Yeah, tell me about it."
"No need, bro. Just gotta roll with it."
"I hear ya. Be cool now."
"You, too."
"See ya."

And suddenly, a full minute of your life is gone, and you've gained precisely nothing from it. And that assumes YOU are one of the two [cough] speakers quoted. This isn't dialog. It's a ping pong volley of mindless clichés knocked back and forth almost as if *communication* were actually taking place. Mutual nods would have accomplished the same thing, plus they'd have contributed to the circulatory well-being of both parties. But this drivel? Ick. **Do Not Put This In Your Story!**

As storytellers we must strive to create *verisimilitude*--the appearance of reality. Because "real" reality is usually boring, and boring is the last thing you want your fiction to be.

Okay, but maybe it's important for Joe and someone else to meet so that a plot point can be established or developed. F'rinstance: Joe can't be the killer because he was talking to Evinrude whilst the wicked deed was done. That's fine, but take the opportunity to make the encounter entertaining. Even a brief exchange can have some punch. Ergo:

"Joe! How they hangin', bud?"

Joe's eyes focused on the floor, clearly depressed.

"What's goin' on? I've never seen you look so glum."

"They're gone."

Evinrude stared at his old pal, confounded. "What's gone?"

"The family jewels. They fell off during the night. It was--I dunno. I can't talk about it."

"Oh, my God! What happened? How--" He tried desperately not to look at Joe's groin, but the temptation proved too strong, and his friend noticed.

"No, Ev. That's not it. They were in a little bag tied to my dog's collar."

"Your dog?"

"Fluffy. My 100-pound pitbull. Anyone wanting to steal the jewelry had to deal with Fluffy first."

And so on. Hopefully, you're a sharp enough reader to note that there were no speech tags in either exchange--no Joe saids or Evinrude replieds. That's because they weren't needed. You know who's talking. In the second exchange, a couple action tags were employed. They provide details about who does what during the conversation. There's nothing tricky going on here. One guy looks at the floor, the other looks at his buddy's crotch. And yet both action tags supply a little business that makes the dialog more interesting.

The litmus test for dialog--surely you remember your grade school chemistry, right?--is a simple question: **Is this conversation *boring?*** If the answer is "yes," you've got work to do.

The easiest way to pump life into dull dialog is to introduce conflict. And, just between you and me, it doesn't matter how inconsequential that conflict is. As long as there's something to argue, worry, condemn or stress over, your dialog will automatically improve. Make somebody angry, or sad, or bitter, or just cranky. The reason can be either irrational or utterly understandable. This is where your life experience comes into play, take advantage of it! We've all had encounters with folks who were contentious for reasons we couldn't control. Now's the time to make those awkward moments pay some dividends. Use 'em!

Example: somebody cut your character off in rush hour traffic resulting in a fender bender. Or maybe some idiot rolled a double cartload of groceries into the 10-item or less lane, and then fumbled around writing a check in the same amount of time Congress needs to pass contested legislation. Or maybe somebody's kid knocked over a huge display and put the blame on your guy.

Every time you introduce something like this, your readers will instinctively put themselves in the place of your character, and they'll invariably be on the side of the injured party. Never forget: you're the master of the dance! You direct the action; you make the decisions. Give your character a problem, and you'll give your dialog life. And your readers will love you for it.

Try this for practice:

Write a short scene involving two characters: one of them has something to hide, and the other one is eager to discover the secret. Using a male and a female, parent and child and/or a boss and subordinate may help to create tension. You can jack that tension level up further by not revealing the secret. Be sure to stick with only one point of view. Choose one of those two characters and stay in his or her head.

~*~

Chapter 8
Tag--he (or she) is It!

As mentioned before, good dialog isn't real, it just sounds that way. But for reasons that will probably remain a mystery forever, many still learning the craft of writing insist on loading up their dialog with crap, by which I mean adverbs, adjectives, unneeded identifiers, and an endless array of substitutes for the word "said."

Let's get the modifier thing out of the way first, 'cause it's the worst of the offenses. The only time you need to use an adverb or an adjective in dialog (and pretty much everything else you write) is when you've exhausted every possibility for finding an action verb to do the job. Then, it's probably okay. But as my Mom used to say, "Don't make it a habit."

Modifiers tell readers <u>how</u> something is said or done; action verbs <u>show</u> them. It's that simple. Mary *whispered* something is way better than Mary said something *softly*. They get the same idea across, but one paints a picture; the other doesn't. You want readers to *see* your dialog as if it were being acted out in front of them. Modifiers replace actors with stage directions. Who wants that?

So, what's an action verb? For me it's pretty much any verb other than "was" and "were." The other forms of "to be" are suspect, but the real offenders are these two. Avoid them when and if you can.

Next, trust your readers to know who's saying what to whom. If there's any doubt, *then* stick in a speech tag. Something like "Joe said" works well. Try to avoid using Joe's name inside a quote, because it's just lame, and almost nobody talks that way. F'rinstance, the following is really bad form (so bad, I was tempted to show it as ~~crossed out~~); for everyone's sake, don't write dialog like this, ever:

> **"You're kidding, Rupert! I didn't know that. And get this, Rupert, that liver transplant I had? Well, Rupert ol' pal, it turns out I didn't need it after all. You may not believe this, Rupert, but someone just unplugged my brain. Who knew?"**

As bad as that was, this is even worse:

> **"You're kidding," Joe said to Rupert, blissfully. "And that liver transplant I had?" Joe laughed hysterically. "It turns out I didn't need it after all." Joe scratched his head vigorously. "You may not believe it, but someone just unplugged my brain," Joe said. "Who knew?"**

Even if you nuke the three modifiers (blissfully, hysterically, and vigorously) the line still sucks. I'd go with something like:

"You're kidding," Joe said. "By the way, you remember that emergency liver transplant I had? Huge mistake. I should've gone to a real doctor."

There's no doubt about it. Joe, our boss, is an anal retentive moron.

The idea of dialog has been around forever. It was old news when the Greeks pumped it into their plays. Socrates employed dialogs to persuade the ancients to see things his way. But the main idea behind **_dialog_** is two-way conversation. Yes, you can have a dialog involving more than two speakers, but in most cases, you'll only have two. If only one character talks, it's a monologue. Tune into any late night TV show with a host, and you'll get an example. But, since you're unlikely to get a job writing monologues for a network comedian, let's focus on character dialog, and let's practice by using two voices.

There are a host of ways to differentiate those voices. Dialect is a good one, provided it isn't overdone. Toss in an odd pronunciation, a bit of slang, maybe a foreign word or two, and you'll lock in the identification without a speech tag or an action tag. [**Note:** we're talking seasoning here, not poisoning. Keep it light; all you want is flavor.]

"Yo, Tex! Whut're you doin' here in the hood?"
"Had to buy me a new shootin' iron, podnuh."

Watch out for pronouns, especially if the speakers are of the same sex. Use both action tags *and* speech tags, but only when necessary.

"It's getting late," Missy said.
Suzie checked her watch and sighed. "You're right."
"Of course I am," she said. "What else is new?"

Break long passages into smaller ones. Use incomplete sentences now and then. Er, uh, and uhm are perfectly natural, as are lines truncated by the response of the other party.

> "I was dating Mary back then, and--"
> "Mary? The one everyone called 'The Nun?' *That* Mary?"
> Joe blinked. "Who called her that?"
> "Well, uhm-- It's, uh-- Actually, everyone did."

If you're more concerned with the content of the dialog than the format, focus on that first, then go back and make it entertaining.

Try this for practice:

Write a short scene focusing on a conversation between two people who've been dating long enough to be serious about each other. In fact, they're living together. One of them claims to have attended an after-hours business meeting and returns home with telltale signs that the business he or she engaged in was the funny kind, not the 9-to-5 kind.

Keep the speech and action tags to a minimum. Finally, write from the point of view of your gender opposite--if you're a male writer, use the female's perspective and vice versa. Have fun with it!

(Pssst! You say you're a wee bit rusty when it comes to punctuating dialog? It's not uncommon. If you'd rather skip finding and memorizing another bunch of grammar rules, go check out the **Appendix** entry for **Dialog Punctuation--by Example**. Most of the issues you're likely to run into are handled there, with a smile.)

~*~

Chapter 9
Last Thoughts On Dialog

A wonderful writer (my Dad, actually) once told me, "Good reading makes hard writing." And it's true. In order for the words to flow smoothly, a writer has to concentrate on moving from one idea to the next, in a logical sequence, and with proper pacing while at the same time finding new and clever ways to express fairly common ideas and situations. It's not easy. But when it all comes together, it's *oh, so* rewarding.

Writing good dialog is just as hard. If you want it to be good, you have to work at it. Fortunately, there are a number of things writers can use to spot areas for improvement. There are three which plague dialog, and writers who wish to be published need to be aware of them. Treat them like warning flags: **dig here!**

Said-bookisms -- I doubt more than one English class in a thousand ever covered said-bookisms. That's too bad, otherwise a few bazillion people who now use them might have learned to avoid them instead. [sigh]

A said-bookism is simply a speech tag other than "said" or "asked." (Some purists even disdain the use of "asked." Not me!) The so-called alternatives include an array of words that attempt to describe how someone said something. They include but aren't limited to: demanded, declared, murmured, shouted, shrieked, exclaimed, inquired, queried, replied, implied, and whispered. Among the most famous said-bookisms, absolutely *guaranteed* to give an editor hives, are: hissed, huffed, barked, frowned, laughed, sneered, and -- my personal favorite -- smirked.

The second grouping is characterized by impossibilities. Try, for example, to *bark* some critical bit of information. Or frown it. Or smirk it. One might concede that it's possible to *laugh* something, but it likely wouldn't be funny.

"What?" he ~~spat~~ ~~queried~~ ~~asked~~ ~~requested~~ ~~shouted~~ ~~yelled~~ ~~whispered~~ ~~grumbled~~ said.

There's nothing wrong with "said." In fact, it becomes invisible to most readers (which is good). Said-bookisms, on the other hand, tend to slow down the pace and, if used liberally, can ruin an otherwise good scene. They can easily become intrusive and annoying. Use them sparingly.

They are best employed when the dialog's intent might be unclear. For instance: "Isn't that just dandy," he groused, or "Great! Just what I needed," she groaned.

Don't just use an adverb instead! Some writers take the easy way out. They'll substitute an adverb [shudder] for the said-bookism. To wit:

    --Said Bookism: "You think you're so smart!" Mona hissed.
    --Adverbial Tag: "You think you're so smart!" Mona said angrily.

The solution? Write *around* the problem; *show* what's going on: Mona shoved the display so hard it hurtled off the table and smashed against the wall. "You think you're so smart!"

Tom Swifties -- funny if intentional, disastrous if not. It can get worse. There's a breed of adverbial modifiers that almost make said-bookisms seem desirable. These are known as Tom Swifties, named after a popular series of YA books produced continuously since 1910, in which a phrase was linked via pun to the manner in which it was delivered. (Puns, we refined folk believe, are the *lowest* form of humor. The worst puns can drive some people over the edge. It's true. I've seen it!)

Here are some examples culled from a 2009 *New York Times* competition:

> "The Babe has been fired!" said Tom ruthlessly.
> "I dream about a less shapely proportion," said Lola figuratively.
> "Oh, I dropped my toothpaste behind the sink," he said, crestfallen.
> "The unemployment rate has increased again," Tom said laboriously.
> "Angelina Jolie isn't pregnant," said Tom unexpectantly.
> "I adore hamburgers," he said with relish.
> "I'm never on time," Tom said belatedly.

The point? You don't want readers to start laughing in the middle of your prose (or memoir) because of an ill-considered phrase.

Lastly, avoid the King Kong of wretched said-bookisms, the 500-pound gorilla squatting in the parlor: "But Mona, *darling*, I love you!" he ejaculated.

Try this for practice:

Just for giggles, make up your very own Tom Swifty, then quickly hide it where no one will ever see it. Or rewrite the sentence in some form you might actually use. Now, wasn't that fun?

~*~

Chapter 10
Bang Starts!

You're sitting in front of your computer, drumming your fingers on the keys as your coffee cools, and the remaining portion of your hastily grabbed writing time is dissolving like an ice cube under a sun lamp. You grow more agitated with every passing second. You can *hear* your precious time drip-drip-dripping down the drain. And yet, you don't have a clue where to begin.

"TASTES LIKE CHICKEN!"

What you don't realize is that you're at the perfect starting point! You can begin *any* kind of story you want. And best of all, you have the opportunity to start it with a Bang. Here's the secret: **merge something commonplace with something unexpected**.

You're familiar with the technique; it's the fundamental element of almost every joke ever told. Consider the old stand-up line: "I met a guy in the soup line the other day. He said he hadn't had a bite all day. So I bit him." [Cymbal crash] Or, how 'bout Demetri Martin's line: "The worst time to have a heart attack is when you're playing charades."

That's the idea, and with a little effort, a story will evolve from that humble bit of wit. Here are some examples of ten different ways to get a story rolling:

Try using a quotation:

"Don't take yourself so seriously," she said. So I laughed as I killed her.

After hearing, "It's not you; it's me. I'm the problem," at least ten times, Juanita began to wonder if maybe the problem was something else.

Advice could be good. What's the best advice you (or your character) ever received?

"'Clean your gun every day,' the old cowboy said, but he never practiced what he preached. He's buried right over there, beside the dead rustler."

Never juggle when riding a bicycle. Trust me on this.

Try using a simile or metaphor.

I married a vampire.

My job is like an open wound.

Pose an intriguing question:

Why do they always put the biggest butthead in charge?

If beauty is skin deep, how thick is ugly?

Think about the future.

Five years from now I expect to take my father's place as the CEO of Banister Technology. Of course, there's always the chance he won't live that long. Arsenic is funny that way.

Define something, or someone:

I'm friendly and caring. My step-sister, though, was the

poster child for lunacy in motion.

Paint a scene.

I always hated market day in Bridgeport. The sewage ran ankle deep in some places, and we could never afford to set up shop on high ground.

Use a comparison to someone famous (or infamous).

Jeb Dooley was every bit as clever as the Three Stooges or Wile E. Coyote.

Dorna had the looks of an angel and the personality of a Doberman pinscher.

Dilemmas offer great opportunities.

So little time, so many banks to rob.

One should never arrive late when summoned by a mob boss, or his girlfriend.

Make up an anecdote.

It's been twenty years, and the memory is still fresh -- the rock music, the odor of suntan lotion, the heft of a gallon of margaritas. Who wouldn't remember a funeral like that?

Try this for practice:

Write a half dozen one-liners. Intentionally contrast something ordinary and plain with something wild, strange, racy or provocative. Once you've got 'em piled up neatly, review them. Find the one that offers the best opportunity for a story, and then expand it. (And save the others for a rainy day.)

~*~

Chapter 11
Welcome to the Idea Mine

The process of creating character motivations, actions, and consequences naturally demands ideas, and this is where weak, uninspired and/or derivative plots evolve. ***I rarely trust the first idea I have for anything***. I urge all writers, and most especially beginning writers, to adopt this attitude.

Idea mining generally means digging deep to get at the "good stuff." Ideas found in the topsoil are those that anybody is likely to have. They're rarely original, and readers will easily recognize where they lead. Digging down below the topsoil gets you into richer territory. Ideas found here will likely work for most readers. Alas, they're very likely to be old hat for editors, agents and manuscript buyers. These folks have seen a _lot_ of second layer stuff, and chances are, anything you find there won't be original to them.

That means if you want to find something unique, you have to dig **way** down, through the subsoil, and into bedrock. And when you get there you'll likely have to chip away at it until the gem you need gets knocked loose. It's work--a helluva lot of work--but it's worth it. This is the zone that generates plot twists no one sees coming. It's where motivations don't just feel right on the surface; they resonate all the way through a character, and the actions the character takes as a result will both intrigue and engage readers.

For example, let's assume I've decided to write a romance, and I'm determined to use the time-tested meme of "boy meets girl; boy loses girl; boy gets girl back."

You and I will probably never extract the same gems from the bedrock of the idea mine, and just because I find something doesn't mean it's the best or the only gem available. Hopefully, you'll find something much better.

First, I need to tackle the boy meets girl part. I could opt for easy--they were sweethearts in school--or I could go the opposite route--she's a nun, and he's a gang-banger from the worst slum on Earth; they meet in the emergency room of a charity hospital where he's being treated for a gunshot wound sustained in a drive-by shooting. Or maybe I'll find something in-between: she's an exotic dancer hired to entertain at a bachelor party he attends. Obviously, there are a gazillion variations available, but readers have seen almost all of them, so I'll have to dig deep to find something original. Maybe they meet at a special school for deaf mutes. (How's *that* for a challenge!)

Obviously, how they meet will impact the how and why of their mandatory separation. Again, finding the unconventional will require effort. In scenario one, my first impulse would be to have one of them move away. Yawn. [Insert your fave cliché about trite plot points.] Better to have one of them kidnapped by terrorists, a crazed school board member, or aliens from the seventh planet.

In the nun/gangbanger scenario, a rival gang could abduct her; a crusading district attorney could target her, or the person in charge of her Order could ship her off to tend Ebola patients somewhere on the "Dark Continent." No? Okay, maybe something happens to *him*-- like prison, or paralysis, or conversion to Islam. Again, choices abound, even though the basic plot hasn't changed since the earliest cave dwellers gathered around a fire to tell lies, impress cave babes, and entertain each other.

How in the world will these star-crossed lovers be reunited, thus fulfilling the third leg of the plot stool? [Ew--he said *"stool."*] I don't have a clue. But I can guarantee I'd grind a heap of bedrock before I worked it out.

Try this for practice:

Take a shot at coming up with a "boy regains girl" ending for one of the scenarios above. See how creative you can be. And, if you're feeling uber creative, come up with endings for all of them.

~*~

Chapter 12
Who *Are* These People?

It's not just a question of who they are, it's also about where they came from. And just who am I talking about? The players in your book. They come in all flavors and sizes, but there's a general breakdown to which I'm quite partial. I think of 'em as the Three Vs: **Villains**, **Victims**, and **Vigilantes**. I've covered the topic before, on-line, in detail, but I'll hit the high points here.

For now, let's concentrate on the basics....

Probably the biggest misconception beginning writers have

about characters is that people care what they look like. Unless one particular physical attribute exists which makes one character or another quite extraordinary, there's little to be gained by writing detailed descriptions of hair and eye color, height, build, sleeve

length, shoe size or any of the rest. What makes a character good or bad isn't how they look; *what matters is what they do and how they act.*

This doesn't mean one can't have character diversity. I'm in the midst of writing a series of novels about a two-foot tall native American Indian. In the third volume, Mato, my very short hero, shares page space with a pair of extremely large "normal" folks in addition to the regular ensemble cast. But other than him, they're all people you might bump into at the Piggly Wiggly, or your local hardware store. (Full disclosure: I populate my **dark** fiction with characters I've seen in Wal-Mart.)

There's a reason I rarely offer more than a few words about the way my characters look: *readers see themselves in the roles of characters they like.*

A good writer will make such self-casting easier by *not* dictating too many details. If your hero is a ruggedly handsome male, and/or your heroine is an unusually attractive female, you've probably provided all the essentials a reader needs to role play. My aim is to help every reader gaze through a pair of rose-colored glasses and "see" themselves acting out the juiciest bits in all their vicarious splendor.

If, however, a writer continually harps on Dudley's chiseled jaw and massive biceps, or darling Nell's petite waistline and enormous, cerulean blue blinkers, readers will have a harder time fitting themselves into those roles. And I mean that in the most literal sense.

How then, does one develop good characters? One way is to begin with a character stereotype and then fashion traits and idiosyncrasies that make the

player unique. When you look at your cast, try to vary the mannerisms and voice of each one. They shouldn't all look, act and sound the same, unless you're writing about robots. And even then, one of 'em ought to be different. Otherwise, where's the story?

The key to making characters interesting is to make them "human." And while it sounds odd, this dictum applies to aliens and animals, too. In other words, give your characters admirable traits *along with* his or her flaws. It'll take a little time, but it's worth it.

You want examples? No problem. Make your villain dependent on a particular kind of Girl Scout cookie, or hook your vigilante on a TV game show. Let these predilections impact a scene or two pushing the character to one side or the other of the Try/Fail divide. The nuttier the flaw the better, I think. Because those things are likely to give your character *verisimilitude* -- the touch, taste

and feel of reality. Imagine a player who can't pass up his or her own reflection without stopping to admire it.

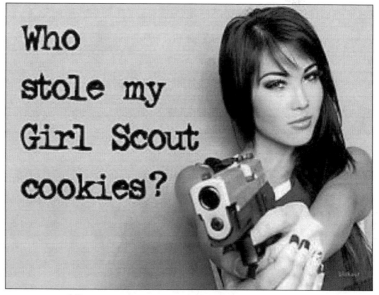

Who stole my Girl Scout cookies?

Here's something to consider before launching a character who is way over the top strange: they tend to work best as bit players, the kind often referred to as "spear carriers" (from the

49

old sand and sandal film epics in which a brawny warrior type always accompanies the hero or heroine. These brutes rarely speak or do much except pose and/or die on cue). This includes anyone wearing a red shirt in a "Star Trek" production.

Wait. What, exactly, is "way over the top?" I'd say any character driven by extremes that defy common sense -- like someone who revels in body piercings, or muscles, or I dunno -- anything! If you need examples, do a quick internet search on extreme [fill in the blank].

Try this for practice:

Think of a stereotypical character--a doughnut-eating cop, a hooker with a heart of gold, or a banker who acts like a pre-ghost Scrooge for instance--and write a few paragraphs detailing some encounter they have with a character who's very much like YOU.

Once you're happy with it, rewrite the whole thing showing how the player you made up varies in at least two significant ways from the stereotype with which you started. (And no, you may not change yourself!)

~*~

Chapter 13
Help--All My Characters Suck!

It happens sometimes. A character you think has potential turns out to be a white bread bore. And as we all know, boring is *bad*. You might be able to write flawless prose; your descriptions might be crisp and insightful; your plot might be completely unique, but if the characters driving it are ho hum, their sleep-inducing presence will contaminate all the lovely bits and turn your masterpiece into a litter box -- one that desperately needs changing.

So, how does one turn bland into dandy? Start by recognizing the most basic truth: ***doing something is always more interesting than doing nothing***. If your characters are boring, it's probably due to a lack of action. This harkens back to chapter 2 wherein we explained that characters must have a **motive**; they must **do something** because of it, and no matter what they do, there will be **consequences**.

Motives aren't that hard to create. Ohio State Professor Steven Reiss has proposed a theory that nearly all human behavior is guided by 16 basic desires. (See **Appendix**, or you can read more about it on line.) For novel writers, we can get by on more general terms: **All characters have needs, wants and desires**. If they don't, they're department store dummies -- mannequins.

The trick is to make those needs, wants and desires *interesting*. One method is to push tepid motivations to extremes. Instead of being hungry, poor Dolly is starved. Instead of being sad and lonely, Fred is isolated and bitter. Instead of being disappointed, Penelope is outraged. Almost anything can be made extreme, and extremes lead inevitably to action. The cardinal rule to remember here is that characters may be obsessed *without* being insane.

Joe sees Molly. She's everything he ever imagined in a girl. Is he content to daydream about her, or does he try to develop a relationship? If Joe finds the courage to approach her, how does she react? Does she laugh at him? Ignore him? Go all goofy? How does Joe handle it? Does he collapse into a wall flower or does he morph into a mouth-breathing stalker complete with a tattoo and a shrine in her honor? Aren't you the writer? Figure it out!

But wait! What if Molly *isn't* really special? What if her self-esteem is so low, she can't tell that she's attractive? How might that drive her? Does she curl up on the sofa and eat gallon after gallon of Rocky Road ice cream while bemoaning her situation, or

does she join the gym, get a makeover, and work out until she can model yoga pants for a living?

What if _her_ desire to look good becomes an obsession? How does she fund it? How does she explain it? Where does it take her?

What are superheroes if not regular folk taken to an extreme? Yet, comic book heroes are hugely popular. I'm not suggesting you give any of your characters super powers, but you should give them *something*--how 'bout a focus, a reason for changing the status quo. Most books have an inciting event, a trigger which starts the plot ball rolling. It doesn't have to be an earthquake or an attack by aliens from the seventh planet. It could be Joe waking up one morning and deciding he's tired

of being a wallflower. Bingo, he swears off stalking, tears down his Molly shrine, and carts it all to a landfill (where he's spotted by someone who knows Molly and can make Joe's life miserable by ratting him out).

Action begets action. Complication drives creativity. Mannequins may look good in a certain light, but they'll always be dummies. Your readers deserve more.

Try this for practice:

Think of a comic book superhero who appeals to you and write a paragraph or two describing how they'd get by *without* their super power(s).

~*~

Chapter 14
Voice: Not Just Throat Clearing

What is it that makes the work of one writer "better" than that of another? If all else is similarly competent--grammar, punctuation, spelling and mechanics--what elevates story "A" above story "B"?

One could argue that plot, characterization, setting, and verisimilitude are the aspects which give a story lift. And yet, I've read--and *written*--plenty of tales that didn't soar despite having all those noble attributes.

In my heart of hearts, as an old friend used to say, I believe it's the quality of a writer's voice that makes the difference.

Voice? Wait. Whut?

A writer's "voice"--to me, anyway--is the quality which truly distinguishes a written work. And it's more than just the sum of its parts. Voice is what gives one set of words power where another set of words merely conveys information. Consider the artfully presented sentence below (attributed to Ernest Hemingway, among others):

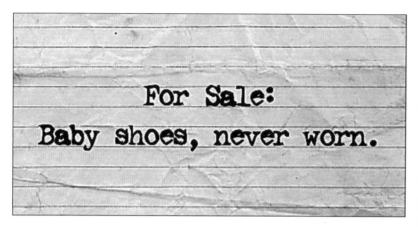

For Sale:

Baby shoes, never worn.

The line operates beyond the obvious. It evokes memories and stimulates the imagination. Six lousy words! But is that an example of voice? Yes, albeit not a very good one. That line may be good, evocative even, but so is: Jesus wept. Neither is quite long enough to become a bestseller on its own. A story needs more, a beginning, middle and end, at least. Voice is what makes those constituent parts less visible and more absorbing. Voice takes the commonplace and makes it not just readable, but special.

Where does this magical stuff come from? In a word: experience. You'll have to do a heap of writing before you'll find your own. But once you've grown comfortable with the way you stack up subjects and verbs, you'll have established a foothold on your voice. Your manner of expression, your determination to dodge clichés, your pacing, the way you adapt sensory text to your will--all of it shades your unique voice.

There's no recipe for quality prose. You can't check off ingredients as you lob them like hand grenades into your story. Try to imagine someone writing that way....

Hey! See this sentence here? It's got pathos, by cracky. And that one over there: it's loaded with imagery; we're talkin' wasabi cheese fries, fer cryin' out loud. Now I'll just sprinkle in a little pacing, maybe some sexy dialog, and something funny. Wait! I've got it: a fart joke. 'Cause just about everybody loves fart jokes. And then--

At some point in your writing efforts, you'll cross into a comfort zone. Getting the right words down, in the right order, with the right embellishments, will become second nature. Your work will have a feel to it that might be emulated, but never duplicated. You'll still have to fix mistakes, 'cause those never go away, but you'll have a much sharper eye for them. You'll catch 'em faster, and fix 'em faster, too. It'll all be a part of what makes up your voice.

You've just got to keep working at it.

In lieu of an exercise to test your grasp of "voice," which I couldn't figure out how to conjure anyway, why not skip to the **Appendix** and try your hand at the **Descriptive Writing Challenge**. Who knows, you might find your voice in there somewhere.

Chapter 15
Why You Need "Good" Bad Guys

If you don't take your bad guys seriously, how can you expect your readers to feel differently? We're talking about **villains** here, and for most adult fiction, two dimensional bad guys like Snidely Whiplash rate no better than what they are: cartoons. Real villains ought to be capable of inducing nightmares.

In comedic films, a bungling bad guy might be worth a laugh or two. The film "Home Alone" demonstrated how two complete idiots could provide slapstick humor for about 60 seconds of a 90-minute feature. Try that in an adult novel, and your readers will dispose of your work like sushi from a filling station. Worse, they'll remember your name, and when it shows up again, they'll treat you like a hitchhiker with a chainsaw. How's that for irony? What you took all too lightly, they'll take quite seriously.

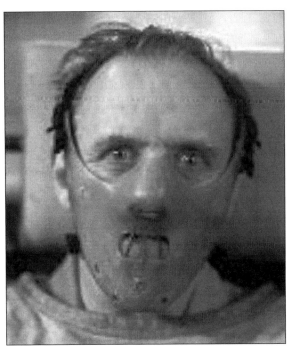

So, no paper tigers. If you're going to put a villain in your book, make sure he's worthy of the designation. Allow him to do despicable things. You have to be mindful of your target audience, obviously. Darth Vader didn't run around cutting the heads off of puppies, but no one ever doubted he'd be capable of it. For the most part, the bad things he did were visited upon his subordinates. Sure, he loped off Luke Skywalker's hand, but he cauterized the wound, and Luke was fitted with a prosthesis anyone would be proud to have. Contrast that with what Peter Pan did to Captain Hook. Who's the bad guy now?

Sorry. 'Nuther cartoon reference. But at least Hook isn't two-dimensional. He's a "real" bad guy. Seriously, if a villain makes little kids walk the plank, how can he not automatically qualify as nasty? C'mon! Geez.

Assuming you're working on a novel rather than a cartoon, you're probably going to need to spend some time figuring out why your bad guy is so rotten. Was he born that way? It's possible, but unlikely. Without getting into the whole environment vs evolution issue, writers will do themselves -- and their readers -- a valuable service by investing enough time in their characters to understand the driving forces behind them. This absolutely includes bad guys.

Nowadays, looking at the news, we can't help but laugh at the idiots who rob stores while wearing uniforms with name tags. "Hi! I'm Jerry, and I'm here to steal your stuff." *[Siren. Blue lights. Click of handcuffs. Clang of cell door. Crack of gavel.]* "See ya in ten years, Jerry baby." If you put that nonsense in your novel--as anything other than a humorous aside--you're begging your readers

Last known photo of Bob

to quit reading. They don't have to invest time or money to hear about idiots. The world provides a never-ending parade of morons who can't think through a crime any further than "Gimme the cash!"

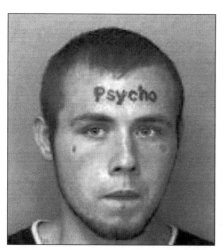

Then they run off down the street with the blinky lights on their discount store sneakers marking their passage. "Yo! Follow me to my secret hide out!"

Oy.

Please, don't let your bad guys be stupid. They don't have to be evil geniuses, but they ought to have enough smarts to intrigue a reader. Let them figure out how to avoid the easy mistakes, at least.

And give them something to make them different. Stereotypical bad guys are as tedious as it gets. We've all seen 'em: the doughnut-munching cop who takes payoffs, pimps (who, no matter what, are all the same), spoiled rich kids (male or female, doesn't matter), dirty politicians, etc. We expect certain behaviors from these characters, and any significant deviation makes us instantly suspicious. Why not use that suspicion to our advantage? Maybe the stereotype is merely a cover for something that's worse?

59

'Course, then there are the stereotypical differences: terrorist, serial killer, demonic possession. There are many others, so picking the one thing that differentiates *your* bad guy from all the rest won't be easy, but it'll be worth it. You'll have to devote some *serious* thought to how your beauty pageant winner turned to chainsaw mayhem or how your Sunday School Teacher of the Year somehow turned into a kidnapper and a cannibal. But just think how much fun writing *those* stories will be!

Isn't it time you got busy?

Try this for practice:

Write a paragraph or two about the worst villain you can think of. Give an example of what makes him so utterly awful and repugnant. But be sure to include something to suggest he or she has at least some tiny shred of decency.

Chapter 16
Death To Weasel Words!

Some folks think weasels are kinda, you know, cute, or something.

What the hell is a weasel word? And how could there be more than one? Sadly, there are almost too many to count, and like their cuddly namesakes, weasel words appear soft, sweet and quite unremarkable. The problem is what lurks beneath that cute exterior: **boredom!**

Weasel words are simply watermarks for timid writers. Using them proves a writer lacks confidence. Who's going to argue with you for saying a girl is "rather" pretty, or a guy is "sorta" handsome, in a wimpy kind of maybe he is and maybe he ain't way.

Spare me! Spare your poor readers, too. They don't want to deal with approximations. If your bad guy has all the clinical appeal of a junk yard toilet, say so! If your heroine is thin and pale and in need of a transfusion, don't tell us she's "a bit" underweight, "perhaps" in need of a tan, and "probably" anemic. **Bleah!** Get on with it already.

The biggest problem with using weasel words is that they're comforting. They don't say things so much as they "suggest" them. In other words, by using them, we surrender the strength and shock value of saying what we really mean. Consider these two descriptions:

So, cut to the chase already! Forget "almost" and "nearly" and "sorta" and "rather" and all that other empty bullshit.

1) Glenard is a damned vampire, but instead of sucking out your lifeblood, he extracts all your energy and leaves you not only emotionally drained but faint, frazzled and woozy.

2) Glenard is the kind of guy who leans on the strengths of other people. He's a bit needy, and he seems to approach his friends like some kind of supplicant, begging their attention, and when he gets it, tends to absorb it.

Are we even talking about the same guy? Understand, after reading selection #1, I seriously dislike Glenard, and I've never even met him. After reading selection #2, I'm getting angry at the author. Is he really so shallow he can't see Glenard for the bottom feeder he so obviously is? Which one would you prefer to encounter in a book--someone who might, you know, just possibly be a slime (#2), or someone you know has deep-seated issues and will probably screw up everyone and everything around him? (#1)

If you're not sure, shame on you! Go back and read my rant in Chapter 11 on the need for "good" bad guys.

Now, working from the Glenard/vampire analogy suggested above, do you see how weasel words suck the life out of prose? They're wishy-washy. They waste your time and, even worse, the reader's. Why? Because they muddy the water. They shroud what should be clear in needless noise. Think not? Go back and read example #2 again. Then, compare it with this sanitized version:

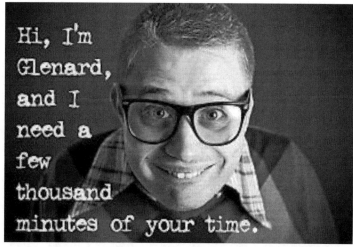

Hi, I'm Glenard, and I need a few thousand minutes of your time.

Glenard leans on the strengths of other people. He's needy, and he approaches his friends like a supplicant, begging their attention, and when he gets it, completely absorbs it.

If you use weasel words enough, you'll wear your readers out, and they'll dispose of your book (or your report, or your short story, or your obit) like an overloaded diaper. Weasel words are useless, boring, empty, time-wasting, energy-sucking, fatuous, blobs of anti-helpful ink--or pixels, or whatever represents the digital equivalent of a skid mark in your literary BVDs.

I hope I've been sufficiently clear on the topic.

Try this for practice:

Look at the first scene/chapter of your novel in progress, or your latest short story, or anything else you've done that's longer than a page. Highlight any and all words that might possibly be of the weasel variety, then get rid of 'em!

(Clichés are a lot like weasel words. They're empty and boring because, well, they're **clichés**--over-used words. Try to avoid using them in any kind of writing, not just fiction. If you think you can handle it, there's an exercise in the **Appendix** you might try. It's called, cleverly enough, the **Cliché Exercise**.)

~*~

Chapter 17
Declare War On "Was"

Let's be clear from the start; I don't like the word "was." It's evil.

That said, I use it. Lord, do I ever. In fact, I probably use it too much. And the really sad thing is: **I know better**. I **understand** the power that one specific, stupid, little word has. Sadly, most writers don't understand it, and I include a wide range of accomplishment when I say "most" writers. Somewhere during our education, whether public, private, or in-home, we should each have been warned about the consequences of using this word in prose, if nowhere else. But I'll wager only a tiny fraction of the English speakers on Earth were lucky enough to get that lesson.

Why is it such a big deal? Simple. Think of the verb "was" as a type of cancer. It creeps into our writing quietly and unobtrusively. It nestles into sentences without the least bit of disturbance, and it occupies the space that ought to be dedicated to a *real* verb. When we look at it, or read it out loud, we just slide right over it as if it weren't there.

The problem is: it ***is*** there! And in 9 out of 10 cases, the sentence could have been written better. Tossing "was" into a sentence relieves the writer of working at making the sentence more interesting. Let me show you what I mean with a few examples.

1- **Mary was a beautiful girl who lived in the house next door.** An okay sentence, I suppose, but quite ho-hum.

2- **Mary, a beautiful girl, lived in the house next door.** Marginally better, and we nuked "was," but the sentence is still bland and doesn't accomplish much.

3- **I often caught sight of Mary, the beautiful girl next door.** Still better, and we get a hint about the observer. But it needs a little more work to be "good."

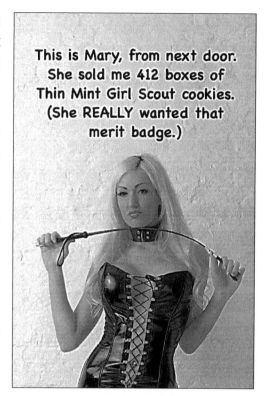

This is Mary, from next door. She sold me 412 boxes of Thin Mint Girl Scout cookies. (She REALLY wanted that merit badge.)

4- **I saw my beautiful neighbor, Mary, seventeen times yesterday.** Now we're on the trail of an actual story!

Let's try a couple more.

A- **The murder weapon was a .38 special, a cop's gun--the same as Joe's. He carried one for years.** [Yawn] This is okay as far as it goes.

B- **The murder weapon? A .38 special. Like Joe's. His hand fit it like a glove.** Better, but the glove cliché is... I dunno... meh.

C- **The murder weapon? A .38 special. Joe instinctively wrapped his hand**

around the grip of his own .38. We not only lost the "was," we added action.

So, how important is this "was" business? It's as important as you wish to make it. Consider scanning something you've written, and highlight every instance of "was." Then, go back and see if you can "write around" the word. Revise the sentence until it doesn't need the damn thing. I'm willing to bet a week's pay that the sentence without "was" is better. And 9 times out of 10, I'll be right. Imagine having odds like that in Vegas!

What about the rest of the stative verbs (is, were--any form of "to be")? It's the same issue, just on a different scale. If you only tackle "was" you'll solve 90% of the problem. Do the anti-was revisions often enough, and they'll become automatic. For now, however, try using the word as a warning flare: Look Here, dammit! Here's your chance to write something **interesting**. Someone once said a good writer can figure out how to put a surprise on every page. Why not start with the Was Warning Flares?

Pay attention to them, then **do something** about 'em, and your writing will improve. I absolutely guarantee it!

Try this for practice:

Remember that chapter/scene from your work in progress that you just finished working on? The one you used for the "Seek and Destroy Weasel Word" exercise? Yeah, **that** one. Dig it out.

This time I want you to highlight every instance of the words "was" and "were," and then I want you to write around them. It will probably require that you redraft more than one sentence, but that's okay. Your goal is to have a better read, and this is a great way to start.

~*~

Chapter 18
Yes, but...

I have written hundreds, possibly thousands, of critiques. I have read some really good first drafts, and some that were, well... let's be charitable and say they needed more work. Lots and lots of work, sometimes. But one thing many beginning writers, and some well-established ones, have in common, is a feeling that they need to defend what they've written.

Which, if you stop and think about it, is pretty pointless.

The whole idea behind a critique is that one person reads the work of another and tries to point out the good and the bad. Some reviewers only focus on the things which don't work. That style doesn't suit me as I think a writer needs to know what works, too. Otherwise they may sacrifice something good while fixing something that isn't.

Nobody says, "Yes, but--" about the stuff that works. Maybe that's why I like to point it out. [shrug] Hey, I'm merely human; I can spot the easy way out, too.

Back to "Yes, but--"

When a reader is looking at your work, unless they're doing it in your presence, which they shouldn't--ever!--they won't get the [cough] benefit of your running commentary about why this hole or that one remains in your plot. They'll be reading along, following the story right up to the point where the toddler slays the kidnapper with a neatly executed karate chop.

"That's just stupid!" the reader says.

"Yes, but I saw that very thing happen on EweTube, or maybe it was on 'The View.' Whatever. Sometimes little guys can do that stuff."

Depending on how much the reader loves the writer (or how much money the former owes the latter) the reading will end soon, a victim of "Yes, but--" because if the writer had anyone read the piece during development, the same comment would almost surely have come up. And just as surely, the writer would have deflected it with "Yes, but."

So sad.

The essential thing for writers to remember, is that critiques and reviews are **opinions.** It doesn't matter if they're doled out by a well-meaning relative or friend, a professional editor or the Pope. You can accept or reject any such input. The only response required of you is, "Thank you for your time. I'm going to consider everything you've suggested. May I buy you a drink, or pay for a massage?"

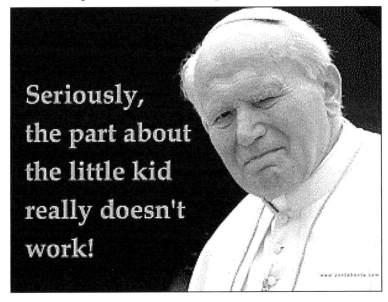

Actually, the third sentence above only pertains to professional editors. You know, folks like [ahem] me.

Just understand, that no matter who looks over your stuff -- and you really should have a variety of different readers check it out -- if more than one touches on the same issue, it's probably worth addressing. And not with "Yes, but." Just fix it, whatever it is. Swallow your pride and/or your faith in EweTube and/or "The View."

Just fix it.

Without the "Yes, but--"

Try this for practice:

Look around the writing class you're in, or at the members of your writing group, or--if you're hopelessly on your own--someone you can trust to tell you the truth, no matter what. Then, ask them to read all or part of your current work in progress. Tell them you want to know only the BAD stuff. Have them focus on and tell you what doesn't work, no matter how hard it is for them to do it. Convince them your skin is so thick it's impervious to any barb they may use on you. You may have to pay them, but it'll be worth it.

When they finally come through with their criticism, listen to it and try not to show any reaction save gratitude. Later, maybe even much later, when you've cooled off, review it again and decide whether or not it's justified and if you need to make any changes.

~*~

Chapter 19
Stop! Don't Answer That!

I care deeply about my audience. I really do. I want everyone to live long lives, read all my titles, and tell their friends about them. The irony is that in order to develop such ties, I have to treat my readers with cruelty.

"Say whut?"

It's true. My goal is to keep the poor dears up all night -- **reading**. How does one do that? How *do* you work folks into such a state that they have little or no

"Spellbinder!"

"Page turner!"

"Intense!"

choice when it comes to turning the page? The answer is embarrassingly simple, and storytellers have been using the technique since they first heard about Cain and Able.

"Couldn't put the darn book down. Kept me awake all night!"

You keep readers on the hook by building suspense, and you accomplish this by posing questions that never get answered, or at least not right away. In most cases, you don't even have to pose the questions. Readers do it for you!

70

Anyone who's ever been deeply *into* a story will recall wondering how in the world a character would survive whatever dire predicament the author plunged him or her into. Really good writers can amp this way up. Some readers seriously agonize over what happens to fictional characters. That calls for exceptionally good writing. But it also calls for smart plotting. Good writers give themselves ample opportunities to change scenes, point of view characters, and pacing.

For some reason, however, many beginning writers completely miss what eventually becomes obvious: if you tell your reader everything right away, you'll have nothing left to tell. Stories grow shorter as deeper secrets are revealed and more questions are answered. Why that should come as a revelation to some has always puzzled me.

So, don't do it 'til you have to!

Let's say you've opened your story with something as innocent as the delivery of an unexpected letter or parcel. The immediate questions, of course, are what's in it, and who sent it. These two questions, at the very least, must NOT be answered! Why ruin a perfectly lovely bit of suspense when you can stretch it out for a page, a scene, a chapter or more? Be content with making the object in question more mysterious. What can you say about the delivery? How does your point of view character react? Is he surprised, agitated, angry, apprehensive, appalled? Does your heroine feign any knowledge of it, try to burn or bury it, send it back?

What you need to be looking for, of course, is motivation. Why does a particular player act the way she does? Once you've settled on something, or several things, you can go about the rest of the story knowing you'll reveal what needs to be revealed in good time -- and that would be when it suits you best. But that point is almost never right off the bat.

Try this for practice:

Write a story opening that features the delivery of a package. Make it as mysterious as you can, and not just about the *appearance* of the package. Did it arrive under the cover of darkness? Is there any way to tell who sent it, and why?

Does the recipient instantly recognize the handwritten address or something about the way it's wrapped? Do your best to construct mysteries, questions your reader will be asking herself over and over as she reads.

~*~

Chapter 20
A Break from the Nitty-Gritty

A short while ago, I read an article by Carl Zimmer in the *New York Times* on-line edition about research recently done in Germany to find out what parts of a writer's brain contribute the most in the creative process. (Full disclosure: I've long believed that two things contribute the most to this: deadlines and poverty, but not always in that order. Most of us who can put off the real work of sitting down and hammering stuff out, will almost invariably do so.)

Here's where you can find the original article in case you need to read it for yourself (suddenly, you don't trust me anymore? Was it something I said?):

http://www.nytimes.com/2014/06/19/science/researching-the-brain-of-writers.html

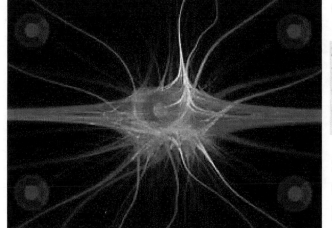

Synapse firing. Imagine a bazillion of these puppies going off in your head every time you dream up a new scene.

So, what happens upstairs when we actually do write something? What parts of our brains kick in, and why?

According to the German study, prolific writers have different internal reactions than those who write less frequently. Both groups may be absolute idea machines, but those who write a lot activate portions of the brain geared to <u>speech</u>. Those who don't write a great deal activate parts of the brain mostly given to <u>vision</u>.

So, surprise-surprise, writers think in words--both internally and externally-- while non-writers think in pictures. It seems likely that seasoned writers, by virtue of practice and repetition, shift the creative process from images to text automatically while those who haven't done much writing struggle to get what they've seen down on paper.

The difference amounts to the novice coming up with: "She was gorgeous in her sexy, green dress." While the writer generates a description of the low-cut, emerald gown and the redheaded goddess wearing it. There's just no way around practice, folks!

Perhaps of more interest is what happens *inside* the brain of a reader. Hm?

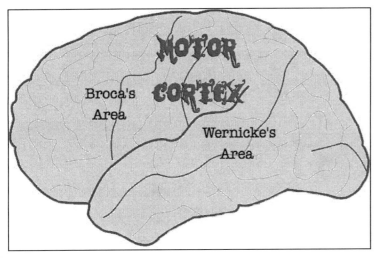

Yeah, there's a whole lot more going on while you're trying not to fall asleep during the PowerPoint, but I don't want to confuse you with too much just now. Stay awake, dang it!

A quick look into established theory yields the following: given a bullet-point list, like those we've all come to love in PowerPoint presentations, the brains of most readers will see action in Broca's Area and Wernicke's Area. This is where language gets turned into meaning. Important, certainly, but not StarWarsy cool.

What *is* way cool is when that same info is converted into story form. That's when the reader's brain gets a jumpstart from the Motor Cortex. Think of it as the Harley-Davidson Area. It's where the stuff that's just been read is converted into something akin to experience. Which do you suppose is more likely to be remembered? Vroom-vroooom!

If you're a writer, and you want to connect with your readers, you've gotta pump some fuel into the Harley Area. You do that with sensory stuff. Let readers know how that sexy green dress <u>felt</u> against the redhead's satiny skin. What her hair <u>smelled</u> like. What her lips <u>tasted</u> like. What... Whatever! We'll take a much deeper look at sensory writing in the next chapter.

Okay, brain surgery's over for today. Go write something.

Vrooooooooooooooom!

Try this for practice:

Relax. There's no writing exercise this time. I want your brain fresh and fluffy for the next topic.

~*~

Chapter 21
Writing for the Nose

Seriously? For the nose?

Yep. It may not be the fastest route to the brain, but it's pretty darned quick. Smells are triggers that can set off a variety of responses. Don't believe me? Try giving two seconds worth of thought to something called "that new car smell."

I can hear the synapses in your brain firing now. Or maybe it's just the clatter of my fingers on the keyboard. Who knows? And while we're asking esoteric questions, what does all this have to do with writing?

Puh-lenty.

Most of us get our information visually, and there's nothing wrong with that. We sometimes toss in sounds, too. Also good. We know what explosions look and sound like. But if we really want to bring an image to life, we need to add an aroma. For things that go **BOOM**, the smell of cordite (which fell out of favor around the end of WWII) is often cited. That gets translated somewhere between tip of nose and temporal lobe as the smell of burnt gunpowder. And miraculously, the explosion you've been describing takes on an added dimension--and it's all in The (Other) Promised Land: ***your reader's head***.

For years, realtors sponsoring open houses would make sure someone baked bread or cookies on the premises, often several times a day. Why? Because everyone knew that the smell of such things meant "home." [Cue "The Waltons" theme] Sadly, few people actually do any bread or cookie baking at home these days, and the practice has largely been abandoned (with no apparent effect on our collective waistlines).

Fragrances are important, and for writers who want to pen memorable settings, the sense of smell can't be ignored. It's not difficult, but it requires some thinking, and if all else fails, you could actually visit the kind of place you're trying to describe for an aromatic 'fresher. **Relax. Inhale. Take notes.**

Consider the following list of smells. Anyone who dares to wear the "Writer" label should be able to conjure a way to work all of these into appropriate settings. And when they do, those descriptive places will have a much better chance of coming alive for readers:

- **Puppy breath**
- **Gasoline**
- **A baby's head**
- **Smoke on clothing**
- **Chocolate**
- **Bacon**
- **Freshly brewed coffee**
- **Pizza**
- **Vanilla**
- **Burnt microwave popcorn**
- **Christmas trees**
- **Cigarette butts**
- **Bus exhaust**
- **Grandma**
- **Raw sewerage**

Obviously, the list isn't meant to be inspiring. For most folks, however, each of these smells is wired to one or more memories, and just reading them will send a tiny surge of electricity ripping through the reader's cognitive connecting tissue to revive dormant thoughts of past experiences. Pupils will contract, fists will tighten, throats will go dry, breathing will change--and the sensory bits of those remembered moments will merge with your scene. As if by magic, your reader will not simply translate your words into an image, they'll *experience* it. Eat your heart out, Gandolf, you old fraud!

Aw g'wan! Try it. What have you got to lose?

Try this for practice:

It's time for a field trip to the nearest deli or pastry shop--in fact, any place that serves fresh baked goods will suffice. And seriously, if there's any way you can arrange to actually go to such a place, this exercise will work significantly better.

Go buy something to eat, maybe get some coffee, tea or hot chocolate, too. Then sit down with your notepad, and pencil, close your eyes, and inhale through your nose. Try to identify everything you smell--pastries, beverages, toppings, whatever. Keep your eyes closed until you've got at least a half dozen. Then, open your eyes and jot them down as fast as you can. Make sure you write enough about each one to prove you smelled it.

Next, take a bite of your pastry and a sip of your drink. Close your eyes again and concentrate on the taste and texture of what you're chewing. Note the flavor and feel of every constituent part. Then write it all down--every bit of sensory information you can remember.

Save your notes for review the next time you write a scene. See if you can do something similar involving your work in progress. Therein lies verisimilitude.

~*~.

Chapter 22
But That's Not How It Happened!

We've all heard the admonition that we should write what we know. And, sadly, some folks still think that's good advice. Trust me when I say it ain't. If it were, there wouldn't be any science fiction, unless it's okay to write about stuff you *know* isn't possible--at least, not yet. The same goes for fantasy of all shades. What do we really know about dragons, elves, fairies and magic? Hogwarts would be considered hog<u>wash</u>, and that would be a terrible shame.

That's the reason folks call it FICTION.

So, forget that nonsense about "writing what you know." Otherwise you're bound to commit the ultimate writing crime: producing something boring.

In what amounts to a corollary to all this, some writers "fictionalize" events they've been closely associated with. Maybe it involves a relative, friend, business associate, former lover, whomever. Sadly, many of these writers can't divorce themselves from *what actually happened.* For them, the girl can't just walk away, because her real life counterpart hung around, refusing to believe her abusive boyfriend wasn't a saint. Or, maybe Aunt Bulimia didn't die from an overdose of chocolate; maybe what did her in was the strychnine that good old Uncle Lester added to her panda poop tea. Or I dunno. The point is--and I absolutely refuse to sugar coat this--no one gives a damn. If the fictional version reads better than "the truth," then screw the truth and go with what you've made up. After all, it's <u>supposed</u> to be fiction, right?

There's absolutely nothing wrong with using real-life events as source material for fiction. Just make sure you're capable of separating yourself from the reality to form your alternate rendition.

Let's take a look at the flip side of this coin. When folks say that "truth is stranger than fiction," they're basing the conclusion on experience. Just because something really happened, doesn't mean anyone would believe a fictionalized version of it. Writers must use common sense, even if it means forcing themselves to do so. (Yes, I know. It's awful what we must do for our art.)

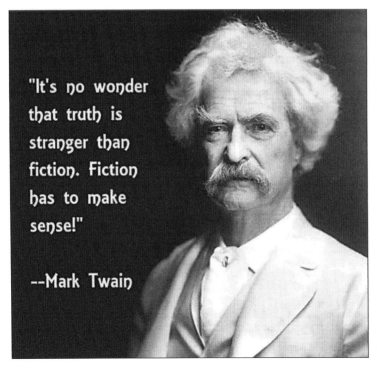

"It's no wonder that truth is stranger than fiction. Fiction has to make sense!"

--Mark Twain

Now consider the sidebar item on the next page, reprinted from the March 22, 2007, **Houston Chronicle**. Can you imagine anyone buying into this criminally stupid criminal if they read it in your book?

Complicating this issue a bit more, let's consider the role of history in fiction. I've always felt it critically important to present a factual version of historical events, unless my goal is to generate <u>an expressly stated alternative</u>.

Getting historical details wrong is a gigantic no-no, except when your whole story depends on it.

For instance, if the core element of your Civil War fantasy is a claim that Union General Ulysses S. Grant actually arranged the assassination of President Lincoln, you can get away with it, and no one will suspect you of an unauthorized release from a psych ward. BUT, if you toss such an absurdity into an otherwise historically accurate portrayal of events, you'll be lucky to retain even those readers to whom you're related. (But they'll forever after look at you funny.)

It's all about judgment. The "rules," such as they are, tend to be rubbery. They bend and stretch like a politician's rendition of "the facts," which we can almost always count on to be as dead-on accurate as a prediction in a fortune cookie.

Good stories may stretch credibility provided they're told skillfully enough. The aim of this book is to help you figure out how to do that. Using good judgment is a skill like any other; the more you practice it, the easier and better it becomes.

A man accused of leaving an El Lago restaurant without paying his tab was arrested a short time later on a trespassing charge by the Lakeview Police Department.

According to a police report, an employee at Gabacho's Mexican Restaurant in the 4400 block of NASA Parkway called police to report the theft.

When officers responded, they learned that the man was seen walking toward a vacant building on the other side of the road after leaving the restaurant.

Police checked the area and found an open door in the back of the building. An officer went inside and called out, "Marco."

The man's name was not Marco, detective Tim Dohr said. Instead, "the officer was trying to inject some humor into the situation."

Police found the suspect after he responded, "Polo."

Try this for practice:

Try to recall an event in your life which you shared with someone you loved. It doesn't matter how long ago it took place. Now, write up that event in third person, as if you were observing someone else in your role.

See how long it takes before you find yourself wanting to make changes to the "truth." Maybe the weather was better, the timing more precise, the food tastier, the participants more--or perhaps less--intoxicated. No matter how strong the urge, make every effort to keep it historically and factually accurate.

When you're done, rewrite the whole thing, changing anything and everything you can think of to make it more appealing as fiction. Move it to a different planet if you have to, or change the players from regular folk to supermen and superwomen. Have fun with it. Stretch the boundaries as far as you can.

Then, re-read both and decide which would appeal the most to the average reader.

~*~.

Chapter 23
Readers as Co-conspirators

Wait. **What?** Readers are supposed to **conspire** with writers? What kinda nonsense is that?

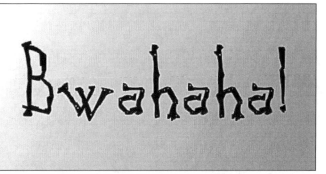

The clever kind. The sneaky kind. The think-ahead kind. It's a strategy any writer can use to enlist the reader's aid in creating settings that resonate in the only place that really counts--deep within a reader's brain.

We are all products of our own experience. If someone mentions a "rustic cabin" but adds no additional description, we're left to conjure an image based on our own familiarity (or lack thereof) with log dwellings. I've seen a variety of such places, from the sumptuous to the squalid. There are log homes nearly as big as the White House or the Taj Mahal. There are also the one-room jobs that housed the likes of Abe Lincoln as a boy.

You remember. We talked about it in Chapter 6.

Readers need more than "rustic cabin," obviously, but good writers will resist the temptation to rely on visual imagery alone. We have to give them more, and the best way to do that is to tap into what they already know.

The problem is, we don't all have the exact same experience. We do, however, have roughly the same sensory powers. So, after specifying the general size and condition of our hypothetical cabin, we can switch to other forms of sensory input to complete the picture.

One of the quickest pathways to the brain is through the nose. It's a short distance after all, and the effects of smell--whether encountered or recalled-- can be dramatic. All we need to do is push the Replay button in our reader's memory. The neat thing is, readers are eager to help us. Words like "musty," "sour," "rank," or "aromatic" evoke memories that can be applied to other settings. ***But the power of recall can be greatly enhanced by specifics.*** Who

doesn't remember the odor of a kid's clothing left to marinate under a bed or in a corner? How about the sudden, sharp essence of hot sauce, the drool-inducing fragrance of freshly baked cookies, or the vile stink of a backed up toilet?

Has the wallpaper sprouted mold or fungus? Have rodents left their mark on the sofa? Did something die in the chimney?

Couple any such smells with your cabin, and the reader will fill in the details. The window dressing, the furniture, the fireplace--all of it will become crystal clear in the reader's head without you having to do anything else. You just set the stage and add enough sensory detail to enable the reader to finish the picture. Best of all, they won't hold you responsible for discrepancies; they'll assume the blame!

The other senses offer powerful inducements to this collaboration too. Touch, especially, works well. Ask anyone who has experienced the feel of a cat's tongue, or who has been outside in shirtsleeves on a winter night in snow country. Sounds, can also do amazing work as evidenced by countless movies. Remember the theme music from "Jaws"?

Or, consider this: Little Maizie is feeling her way down the basement stairs in the dark. She reaches out, her hand lightly touching the wall in search of the

switch. She finds it, and flicks the tiny lever, but nothing happens. The resulting click echoes in the dark. Still, she must keep going. The danger behind her is worse than that ahead, or so she thinks. Each step brings the soft shuffle of slippers on bare wood.

Until a new sound grabs her. It's a low sound, hard, guttural and coarse. She strains to see something--**anything**--in the gloom. And then she hears it again. Closer. And louder. And all she can think of are the tales of the blue-skinned boojums her daddy used to tell. How they lived in the dark. How they ate little girls. How they growled, soft and low, just before they attacked.

Sensory words. Put 'em to work!

Try this for practice:

Write a paragraph or two from the point of view of a blind child, abandoned in a modern department store at Christmas time.

~*~

Chapter 24
"Chunk Style" Writing

Forgive me, please, for a moment of wool-gathering. Whenever I think of "chunks," I can't help but conjure an image of Arnold Stang gazing, drooling, lusting, or in deep contemplation of a hefty cube of chocolate known as a "Chunky."

Given the option, I'd probably unwrap one of those magnificent blobs of dark brown goodness and gobble it down before the start of every writing session. And if I did, I'd likely be the size of a Martian moon. In a healthier context, I believe the "chunk to ultimate mass" idea could rise to meme status among writers. (Hot damn--I've invented a meme!)

When one finally removes all the barriers we encounter just to be able to sit down and write, we're often faced with the enormity of creating an entire work, be it a short story, a novella, or part *N* in a series of books which seemingly has no end. The key to getting over this last hurdle is thinking in smaller terms: **chunks**. You <u>don't have to</u> write the entire epic in one sitting. You don't even need to finish a whole scene.

You only need to produce a chunk of it. That's easy enough. It could be just a **beginning**, wherein the heroine wakes up and smells something awful and peers up into the pearly eyes of a ferocious beast lately escaped from a nightmare of the Qing Dynasty (or her mother-in-law's cooking).

Or it could be a **middle**, wherein said damsel stabs the dragon with the leg bone of a partially eaten unicorn. Or it could be the last bit of the action, where the mortally wounded dragon wheezes its last and lands squarely atop the hapless warrior babe. Not only does this knock the wind out of the girl, but it leaves readers breathless as well, and hopefully panting to get to the next scene to find out if she survives.

Chunks can be any size. The concept applies to time as well as word volume. If you only have ten or fifteen minutes to work on your opus, then write a 10- or 15-minute chunk. Write half the opening. Write the start of the middle. Write one line. **Just one!** Go ahead and spend the <u>entire</u> ten or fifteen minutes on it, but for Pete's sake, **save your work.** Read it again the following day to get fired up about the next chunk, or if need be, the next single line.

Consider the Sistine Chapel ceiling. It took Michelangelo four years to paint, and while he managed to be insanely productive, his genius didn't allow him to produce more than a chunk at a time. At some point, he had to focus on the most obscure details--things which a writer might ignore if under a tight deadline. But it's the detail, more often than not, that brings a story or a painting to life.

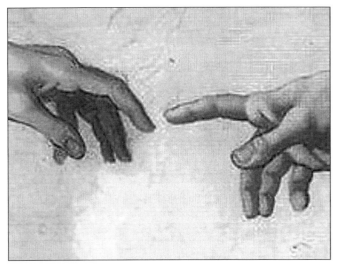

You can get by writing just a tiny chunk, the equivalent of a fingernail on the hand of Adam in the middle of that magnificent chapel ceiling. It's only a piece of the whole, but it's just as worthy as any other chunk.

Whatever you do, don't wait for the muse to put in an appearance. She won't, because she has other plans. And while you may not be happy to hear this, those plans don't include you. Sorry. You're on your own, Bubba.

But take heart! The chunk meme can work for you. Just keep at it. Pile one chunk atop another, whether you grind out a sentence a day or seven chapters a week -- or more. Eventually, you'll get to the end.

Just don't stop. Don't give up. Ever. You can get it done, a chunk at a time.

Try this for practice:

Drop everything. This instant! And write a cover blurb for your current Work In Progress. If you don't have a work in progress--and shame on you if you don't!--make something up. Write a cover blurb for a book you'd *like* to write. Do it now. No excuses!

Chapter 25
Shades and Variations

It occurred to me as I read through some of the stories submitted by my students, that many of them missed opportunities to enhance their work through shades and variations. Like most writers, they were working with a deadline, so I can appreciate the weight of the monkeys on their backs. Who has time for nuance?

But writers **must** make time for it, else why bother writing? Like artists working in any other medium, writers must command the tools of their trade. They must

also develop specific skills, like those required to hunt for nuance--to find the **exact** word that fits a given situation.

Consider the sentence: **Bertram walked down the hall in his underwear**. How many different ways might ol' Bert traverse that stretch of floor? He could saunter, stroll, skip, slide, slouch, stampede, sashay, shimmy or stumble, and he'd only have put a dent in the stockpile of S-words. Best of all, each alternative offers a different shade of meaning for "walked." And yet, each has the power to alter the sentence-- and possibly the whole story--in significant ways.

The range of reaction is wider than you might think. Based on the specifics of the character those words are applied to, readers will react even more differently. Just consider the profoundly different views afforded by the retreating forms of middle-aged, overweight Bertram and that of the reigning Pin-up Girl of the Year. All of a sudden sauntering, strolling, skipping, sliding, et al. generates an even wider range of motion. And thank the Lord for that!

The other benefit of taking the time to select the proper words--and by that I mean **verbs**, words that do the heavy lifting--is the reduced temptation to use some sort of modifier. Nuanced words rarely need adjectives or adverbs. They're superfluous. The verb shoulders the load. You're happy; I'm happy. Shoot, Hemingway is likely giggling and laughing, too.

Here's what I tell my students over and over: "Avoid words that end in **-ly**." Save the shading and variations for words that actually do something, not those that hang around *pretending* to work, like surplus supervisors on a road crew. Spare us all from sentences like: "Bertram walked slowly down the hall in his underwear." I'd much rather read that he played air guitar and accompanied himself with a vocal bass line while maintaining the rhythm with his tap shoes.

Or show me a photo of Miss Hot Pants. Any year will suffice.

Try this for practice:

Pick a character from your current Work In Progress and detail what he, she or it would look like wandering down a hall garbed in nothing but underwear.

~*~

Chapter 26
Hie Thee to the Discomfort Zone

At one time or another, we all must face the prospect of doing something we're not good at. Most recently for me, that moment came when I was asked to make an announcement about an upcoming event at the school where I teach. I realized I needed to do something extra-- something well beyond the ordinary--or my announcement would fall on ears tuned to chit-chat. I'd seen it happen all too often.

So, instead of timidly approaching the podium to go through yet another public service announcement, I dressed up in what I thought would make me look like the absolute King of Swagger. I even gave myself a pseudonym, Slide N. Becool, which I thought had just the right sort of stylish ring to it. Check out the debonair, zoot-suited devil in the accompanying photo. I'm quite sure nothing short of a name like Jarvis Q. Dork would fit better.

91

Then, rather than grab a microphone and natter away, I entered the hall from the opposite end and sashayed through the place carrying on at a volume that would have been heard reasonably well in an NFL stadium--on a Sunday in the fall.

My audience consisted entirely of folks over 50, and they were busy eating lunch with their friends, so getting their attention was no easy matter. It helped that I was willing to make a complete fool of myself. And yes--before you ask--I've had <u>lots</u> of practice.

Anyway, it worked. The conversation level dropped to zilch, and I managed to ad lib my way to the podium. Fortunately, I had a good-natured accomplice who was also willing to provide the sort of repartee that gets a laugh or two. We got several. Probably more than we deserved. I credit the costume.

Now, what could this possibly have to do with writing a novel? Here's the thing: ***it's all about taking chances***. I didn't <u>have</u> to dress like a fool, and I didn't <u>have</u> to act like someone named Slide N. Becool. No one would have said a word if I'd remained my usual, self-effacing, unassuming, gentle mole-like self. But then, I wouldn't have gotten much of a reaction from the audience either.

What you write--and how you write it--works in much the same way. If you refuse to explore *un*comfortable areas, you run the risk of telling the same sort of story over and over. You give readers a sadly reasonable question: Why buy volume two if it's merely a rehash of volume one?

When my good friend, Barbara Galler-Smith, and I were working on our first collaborative novel (**Druids**--a great book, by the way, go buy a copy now), we reached a point in the story which called for a sexy scene. Actually, it required way more than that. It demanded a hot, steamy, page-curling sex scene, one which would have a profound impact on the entire series. Naturally, we had a long and involved discussion about which of us should write it.

Back then we both worked full-time at non-writing jobs. Barb taught science in a middle school; I worked for an airline as a computer programmer and business analyst. The people she worked with were focused on surviving puberty. My co-workers were flight attendants, some of whom may also have been struggling with puberty (but that's a whole different story).

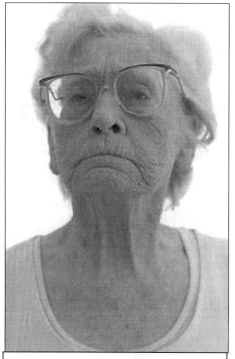

"My students will read it," Barb wailed, quite understandably. "And they'll tell their parents, who will think I'm a sex fiend."

"The hell with that," said I. "My *mother* will read it, and she'll *know* I'm a sex fiend!"

We discussed this impasse at length and finally concluded that my mother, who raised four fairly normal kids, might possibly have some knowledge of **S-E-X**. She might even be capable of reading the scene for its [cough] literary value.

Full disclosure: This is NOT Barb Galler-Smith. Nor is it my Mom.

Geez. Who knew? Anyway, I wrote it. Barb edited it. Edge Books published it, and the rest is history. Your mileage, naturally, may vary. The point is, when it's time for you to write a sizzling sex scene, don't go hide in the laundry. Cowboy up and write the damned thing. Make it as hot and steamy as you can. Ignore that little voice that says "Your kids will think you're crazy," or "Your boss will think you're crazy," or "Your ___ will think you're crazy." Because when it's all said and done, no one cares. Not even ____, whose negative opinion you think means so much right now. It doesn't. So write naked!

You'll survive. And by writing that uncomfortable scene, you'll be a better writer--but only if you give it everything you've got. Don't do it for your spouse, your editor, your beloved rabbi, your dear aunt Beulah or anyone else. Write it because your career depends on it.

Try this for practice:

Write a sex scene involving two characters from whatever story you're working on right now. If that's impossible--because the characters are too young, too old, too infirm, or too something else--pick one who's healthy and pair him or her with a comic book superhero or some well-known character from the stage or screen.

If you simply can't force yourself to write a sex scene, and I realize some folks will never be able to, then think of something unconscionably dreadful to do to the lead character in your current project. Be utterly and absolutely ruthless in this. What the hell, we're only talking about a couple paragraphs. But pretend you might use it in a sequel, and write it the best way you know how.

~*~

Chapter 27
Who Doesn't Love Sex Scenes?

If you're anything like me--human, mostly--and you've spent any time at the beach, you're probably already aware that the ratio of truly beautiful people to the rest of us is, well, pretty damned small. And I mean "beautiful" in the most rudimentary sense: *exterior* beauty. I'm referring to perfect hair, a perfect smile, a perfect body--the works.

So why in the world do we insist on writing about fantastically gorgeous people? Who are we kidding? Not every hero needs to be six foot four, weigh 200 pounds and have a 30-inch waist. Seriously. I could count the number of guys I know who are built like that on one hand. Nah. Make that: one finger.

Ditto for the ladies. I'm pretty sure I found and married the very last perfect gal of my generation, and thank God she still tolerates my presence. But on our last beach trip, I had my worst fears confirmed. Hang on to your hats, people, I have really bad news: Most of us just ain't all that hot.

But you sure couldn't tell that by what we write. According to all the fiction I've seen lately, women are universally slender, often petite, with flowing locks and azure eyes--usually limpid ones, whatever in hell that means. The guys all seem to have lantern jaws and slab upon slab of lean muscle. And when one of those guys climbs into bed with one of those gals... Well, let's just say *miracles* happen.

Yes, yes, I know we're writing fiction, and a desirable element of fiction is fantasy. And certainly, the sex I've been reading about is nothing short of fantastic. Who knew that **tab A** could be connected via **slot B** with such spectacular results? Every time. No matter what--or where. Flawless execution, perfect timing, mutual satisfaction, no remorse, and almost never any procreation.

I'd say "fantasy" pretty much covers all that.

Please don't get the impression I'm some sorta sex scene Scrooge. I've written my share of randy romps that logic dictates are utter nonsense. And I've been told folks generally liked 'em. Which is nice.

But once in a while I'd like to read a bedroom scene that contains something a little more "real." Let's face it, human bodies weren't designed to operate in complete silence, and I'm not talking about someone screaming (moaning, gasping, grunting, or otherwise fulminating) the classic, "Oh God, oh God, oh God!" line.

Sometimes people actually laugh. I'm not kidding. Really--they do! And why not? They're supposed to be having a good time. Heavy breathing is fine, but why couldn't someone burst out in song? Okay, maybe not the "Hallelujah Chorus" or "Row, Row, Row Your Boat," but something melodic in between might be nice.

Or maybe, just once in a while, the fireworks <u>don't</u> happen. I'm guessing that outcome is a lot more common than folks think. And if I'm wrong, who's paying for all those Viagra and Cialis commercials?

In my classes I often use the word **verisimilitude**. It means the appearance of being true or real. Very handy word,

"Darling? You'll never guess what I have...."

"I can't imagine. Will it break through porcelin?"

despite being a mouthful and hard to spell, even when sober. But it's of critical importance when writing fiction. One must focus on creating the "appearance" of reality. How does that apply to sex scenes?

I suspect the answer lies somewhere between the perfection we all wish we had and whatever it is we actually have. A little of this, a little of that, and before you know it, you've got... a casserole! And you know what, casseroles can be pretty darned good. Especially the spicy ones.

Try this for practice:

Write a sex scene that starts out hot and heavy, but quickly falls apart for some reason. Maybe it's the people next door, a wandering opinion poll worker, a telephone that won't stop ringing or something else equally annoying. Turn that sensual romp into something totally unexpected. Have fun with it. Make your characters laugh. Make <u>yourself</u> laugh!

Who knows, you might just stumble across something that'll work well in your next masterpiece.

~*~.

Chapter 28
Don't Tell It Too Soon

That advice sounds more than just a little bit cryptic, but it's important, especially if you're still in the early stages of learning to write fiction, and more specifically, **commercial** fiction. It's a suggestion I first heard from my father-- a damned fine screen writer and director, by the way. He told me to keep my stories to myself, at least until I'd finished the first draft.

I couldn't imagine anything more stupid than that, probably because I was in college at the time and already knew everything worth knowing. Since then reality has given me scores of well-deserved beatings, and I now fully appreciate and endorse the wisdom of his remark and recognize the enormity of the gaps in my knowledge. Sparing the rod did me no good whatsoever.

So, let's say you've got a splendid idea for a story. It's something that's completely yours--a brilliant new concept, a clever approach, an amazing new character, a plot twist so devious no one would *ever* see it coming. You're in high mental cotton at this point. Your synapses are firing like roman candles, and it feels so good you can hardly think about anything else. Your first inclination is to tell someone about it. It's too good **not** to share. You're convinced that anyone you tell will instantly burst with envy for failing to think of it themselves. You're ready to feed off that feeling of utter superiority, and you'll want to tell more people so that they, too, will recognize how insanely clever you are. Right?

Uh... No. It almost never works that way, for a few really good reasons. But rather than shoot down that perfect bubble or put sand in your creative gas tank, let's assume that this idea of yours actually merits all the superlatives I've been hurling about.

After you've blabbed about it to your buds--those who're sober enough to pay attention--and you've cornered your spouse, your accountant, the hairdresser, and all your neighbors, and you've regaled them about your idea, it won't seem quite as neato-keeno as it was before you opened your mouth to talk about it. You begin to shorten the delivery as details which you originally thought essential get sloughed off like bonus dog hair. After a while you'll be down to the proverbial bare bones, and the awesome idea you had--about which you were so elated before--you'll now think of in terms of yesterday's news. It'll be ho-hum, yawn, put-yer-ass-to-sleep, **tepid**. It's not just a store-bought cookie, it's a dull, tasteless, **stale** store-bought cookie which you happily consign to the literary septic tank.

Why is that? What happened to that brilliant bit of creativity, that shooting star of sensation, that riveting rush of realism, that fantastical flash of fable? Short answer: you <u>talked</u> it to death. All the excitement and enthusiasm of discovery dribbled out, a bit at a time, until there wasn't enough left to interest you in writing it down.

So, so sad. Fortunately you can avoid this disaster.

How? Keep it bottled up inside. Let it fester, smolder, percolate, or whatever else your stuff does when it's in mental development. When the time's right, get it all down in actual words and sentences. Write it as fast as you can. Don't worry about pretty. Don't worry about grammar, or spelling, or mechanics. ***Get that magnificent, raw, creative cookie dough <u>down</u>***!

Of course, when you do the first read-through of the first draft--which we all know should be done ***OUT LOUD***--you'll find no end of stuff wrong. But that's okay! It'll still be interesting. You'll massage it and revise it and poke at it and pull on it until it becomes something ***almost*** worth someone else's time to read.

Then, before you show it to anybody, put it away. Let it cool. Work on something else. Go pay bills; wash the dog; mow the lawn; muck out the barn; shovel snow. Do whatever you have to do to cleanse your mind of what you just wrote.

THEN, and only then, you can go back over it one more time, OUT-<u>bloody</u>-LOUD, and fix the stuff you missed before. But understand, you're still not finished with it yet; there will be many more changes ahead, but at least when you finish this pass, you'll have something read-worthy.

At that point you may share it. But be sure to mention that it's still a work in progress, because unless you're an extraordinarily wonderful writer--which, I promise, you ***aren't***, yet--it's going to need still more work before it's ready to print.

Try this for practice:

Take your spouse, significant other, mentor, or best friend out to lunch. Thank them for being there for you, no matter what. Talk about anything EXCEPT your current writing project OR the one you're thinking about doing next. Practice smiling, and don't you dare let them pick up the check!

~*~

Chapter 29
The Little Stuff Matters, Too

Let's say you've reached that point in your latest writing project when you think it's safe to relax. You typed "The End" on it days ago, and you've finally resurfaced after drinking yourself into a well-earned state of oblivion. Life is good. The **Work** is done. You're a verb mongering deity, and you can hear the world revving up the engines on their bulldozers to begin work on the twelve-lane path to your door.

Right?

Well, Binky [cough] maybe not. There's a fairly strong chance that you're not *quite* done yet, no matter what your spouse, parent, gardener, pharmacist or masseuse might suggest. F'rinstance, have you read your opus out loud? All of it? Start to finish?

If not, you've probably already missed at least a scadzillion little things that really, truly--I mean *seriously*--need to be changed. Not because they'll have a great impact on your

UH, NO.

plot, but because they're likely to have a great impact on your reader's patience. It doesn't take long to convince a reader that you're either new at this thing called writing, in which case you don't know any better, or you're too damned lazy to go back and correct the nits and wobbles that make readers groan. Either way, you lose

It takes about a half dozen such missteps to derail the average reader. If they all come in the first chapter or so, said reader will chuck the book and move on to the next one, specifically one <u>not</u> written by the same author. Long-suffering readers, like your Mom or the gargoyle living above your garage, might hang in there longer, but even they will tire eventually.

But, wait, you'll be tempted to say, *my* writing isn't like that! I don't get befuddled by verb tenses, and I use SpeelCheque-Deelux, so there couldn't possibly be any booboos of that ilk, and my vocabulary is like, y'know,

exemplary and stuff, so I'd never, ever, use a word misappropriately, besides which nuance is my muddle name.

[Yawn.] Imagine me delivering a world class Bronx cheer, at a decibel level of about **99** on the Richter scale, replete with a hogshead of derisive slobber.

I'm going to repeat myself here, so pay attention. I wouldn't do it if it wasn't important. ***The little shit matters.*** All of it. The problem is, your brain is hard wired in such a way that <u>you can't see all your mistakes</u>.

I wish this weren't true. I also wish I weighed about 50 pounds less, and that I had to spread my wealth across a thousand banks so I'd never surpass the deposit level insured by the FDIC. Dealing with the small stuff, however, is something I ***can*** do.

Recognizing that we're all afflicted with the same problem is a good first step. Being blind to our own mistakes isn't weird; it's normal. What's weird is **knowing** that we can't see them and **pretending** they don't exist. That's not only vain, it's stupid, because they <u>do</u> exist, and readers will see them, and they'll laugh at you. Behind your back. In the dark. And not even your very bestest, most busomist buddy will ever tell you. Because he or she will be laughing at you, too.

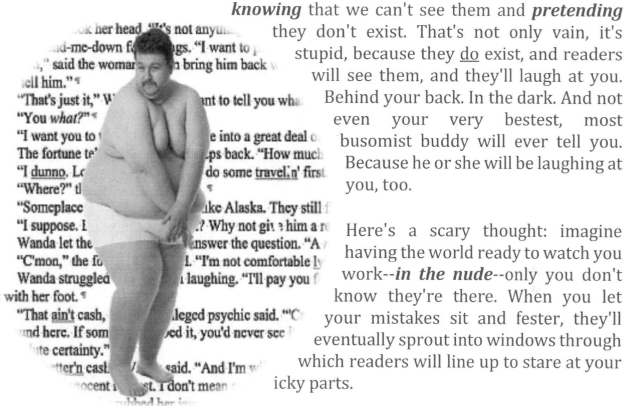

Here's a scary thought: imagine having the world ready to watch you work--**in the nude**--only you don't know they're there. When you let your mistakes sit and fester, they'll eventually sprout into windows through which readers will line up to stare at your icky parts.

You can prevent this--just find the little buggers and gas 'em!

How do you do that? As mentioned previously (so many, many times), read your stuff out loud. Slowly. This will downshift your brain to the speed of your mouth. <u>Saying</u> each and every word will allow your brain to <u>process</u> each and every word. Instead of seeing what should be there, you'll have a chance to see what's really there.

I've known writers who claim to read their stuff backwards. I'm sure that probably works, though the mental gymnastics scare me. But I fully understand the concept. The idea is to make it impossible for the writer to get caught up in the story. If that happens, you're pretty much screwed. From that point on the warts turn into beauty marks and wretched becomes rosy. Trust me on this.

The other most tried and true method of finding your literary lice is to have someone you trust look for them. This means sucking up to people who command two vital strengths: the ability to recognize mistakes, and the willingness to point them out. Such people know a basic truth: it might sting to learn you're not perfect, but it stings a whole lot more to discover the world is laughing at your work, or worse, ignoring it.

Try this for practice:

Before you release your next brilliant piece of handiwork do this:

- Read it out loud, and fix the mistakes you find as you go.
- Find a half dozen readers you trust to check your work. Then fix it.
- Read it out loud AGAIN, and fix the mistakes you find as you go.

Go ahead; hate me now. You'll thank me later.

~*~

Chapter 30
How Much is Enough?

Writers can be very competitive folk, especially when it comes to the topic of production. Like people in any other profession, some writers exaggerate while others are painfully honest.

Dean Wesley Smith for instance, really does crank out a prodigious volume of work. His goal (as stated in his blog) is two million words a year. That's 1000 words per hour, eight hours a day, five days a week, 50 weeks a year. I don't write *quite* that much. [cough]

I also know a couple writers who claim to churn out amazing quantities of prose, yet they publish very little. They can't all be completely full of crap, can they?

Yes and no. Some writers refuse to publish independently. Therefore, they're locked into what used to be called the "traditional" publishing route-- tradition in this case means sending your work to agents or editors with no thought of self-publishing. That's not the way it's always been done, despite what

The Big ~~Six~~ Five:

Penguin Random House
Macmillan
HarperCollins
Hachette
Simon & Schuster

105

the Big Six would have you believe. (Oops, my mistake. I missed another merger. The Big Six is now down to the Big Five.)

There's certainly nothing wrong with having your book picked up by Simon & Schuster or HarperCollins or any other publisher of note. I'll gladly stand and applaud anyone who can traverse the obstacle course that leads to publication in the "traditional" manner. A few people who publish this way will achieve wealth and fame. Their books will be picked up by celebrities and other influential folk, and overnight the writer's names will become the subject of late-night talk shows and book clubs. There will be a bidding war for the movie rights, and editors will complain that they never got the chance to look at any of the manuscripts before somebody else jumped on them.

For most people, however, the real world provides a different scenario. Getting a book into an editor's hands is a difficult and time-consuming process, and even if successful it often results in the publication of a couple thousand paperbacks which will stay on bookstore shelves for a matter of weeks. They will receive no fanfare or publicity beyond what the author provides, and after a couple months they'll be taken off the shelf; the covers will be stripped off and returned to the publishers for credit, and what's left of the books will go into a dumpster. The book will never earn out the author's advance; the rights to the book will forever remain with the publisher, and the author won't be able to sell another book to that same imprint without changing his or her name, because the accounting department will never forget that the first book wasn't a hit. (Thank you, Harvard MBA program.)

I apologize if my admittedly jaded view of the "traditional" method puts a dent in anyone's enthusiasm. I'm merely being realistic. The odds of an anonymous writer making it big on their first novel are about the same as the average college football player's chances of being drafted by the NFL in the first round. It's on a par with the chances of any kid who moves to New York or Hollywood in hopes of becoming a star by standing in line at open casting calls.

The truth is, there are way more gifted people available than the system needs. It applies to publishing, movies, recording, professional sports--just about any field based solely on talent. And the really crazy thing, the thing that makes so many of us scratch our heads or swear or groan, is that so many of the people who "make it" really aren't very good. Many of them just, simply, suck.

But, back to the main point: production. How much do you need to write? How many words should you aim to churn out in a day, a week, or a month? What's the norm? What's reasonable?

If there were a magic number, I'd gladly share it with you. How much one writes depends on the individual and the demands on that person's time. I think two pages a day is a very reasonable target. Others will disagree. If I'm on a roll, I'll crank out a whole lot more than that. If I'm doing my taxes, or taking care of my grandkids, or pulling the ivy out of the trees in my yard, I'm not going to write much of anything.

Oddly, my bourbon consumption will remain fairly steady whether I'm writing, painting the house, building a deck or watching my grandkids play in my pond. If I approached writing the way I approach Kentucky's finest, I'd get a helluva lot more written.

How much should you expect of yourself? As much as you can do. Try to write every day. If you can do two pages, that's awesome. More is better. Less is okay provided you try to make up the difference later. Two pages is about 500 words. The average novel is about 90,000 words. So, at 500 words a day, you should be able to write two novels a year and still have nearly a whole week to just goof off. So, get busy!

~*~

Chapter 31
It's Really *Not* About You

Quick! Raise your hand if you've ever modeled a character in a story on yourself. C'mon, be honest.

Hmm.

Maybe I should have asked for a show of hands from those who **haven't** done it.

Yet. But either way, it points out how common the practice is. And honestly, there's nothing wrong with it. After all, who knows you better than you? Other than your Mom, your spouse, your analyst, and about a dozen others you haven't thought of in years.

(Psst! Send me $10 and a self-addressed, stamped envelope, and I'll respond with your personalized list by return mail. Hurry! Supplies are limited.)

Quite a few of my writing students put themselves in their stories. It's not something I either encourage or discourage, and usually it's harmless. I put a power tool repairman in one of my novels. (**Resurrection Blues**. Awesome story. Run out and buy a copy now!) It felt quite comfy. But I never mistook the character in the book for myself, even though I spent a thoroughly regrettable portion of my life resuscitating dead construction equipment. For one thing, the fictional repair guy was thinner than me and a whole lot better looking.

Typical customers in need of power tool repairs. I did what I could for them, but for some reason, it was never enough. Go figure.

In too many of my student's stories, however, the writers struggle to separate their personal history from their make believe. "But that's what I--oops, sorry. I mean, what *she*--really wore!" or "really did" or "really said" or really whatever. Please, just stop!

Listen up. No one cares. And no one else will ever know, unless the writer tells them, and then they'll care even less. Honest! I'm not kidding.

Back in the day, when I was more concerned with armatures and power supplies than armed assassins and power struggles, I dealt with customers on a daily basis. Some of them were really great people, and I'm reasonably certain some weren't actually human, but none of them was worthy of inclusion in a work of fiction. And neither was I. Which is the whole point. If you need to cast yourself in a story, do so for a reason--because you have some sort of real world expertise, for example. But then get the hell out of the way. Remove yourself, because no one's going to believe you if you don't.

Here's the thing, the real deal, the secret handshake, the magic words, the phrase that pays, the almighty toilet plunger of truth: fiction readers want a rollicking good yarn, that's all. If adding your hard-won life experience will make that yarn better, then do it. If not, don't. Pick a more interesting protagonist, even if it's not a power tool repairman. Spend a little time finding out what kind of cool stuff such a player knows, and work with that. Maybe it's a seamstress, a middle school teacher, or a grocery bagger. It doesn't have to be a mad scientist, a four-star general, or a cover model for *True Romance*. (I know that guy, by the way, and he's so weird you wouldn't want to spend two minutes with him, whether he flexes those massive pectoral muscles or not. Trust me on this.)

Go write something interesting. Something that's not boring. No one can ask for more than that.

Try this for practice:

Think about what you do best, then imagine that you're better at it than anyone else in the entire world. You're so good at it that a sponsor has come forward and posted a challenge: they'll pay $1,000,000 to anyone who can beat you at your own game.

Now, write a story about it. Be a star! Kick the competition to the curb, repeatedly. Until one day….

~*~

Chapter 32
Never--Ever--Shoot a Reviewer

Read that title again, then go ahead and chuckle. You probably think I'm kidding.

Okay, I am. Sorta. But not if you're truly sensitive about your writing. If all you want to hear is praise when it comes time to find out what other folks think of your work, then you've definitely stumbled into the wrong business. Do yourself a favor and quit. Now. Do not think another fictive thought. Ever.

My writing is most certainly *not* "Doo doo!"

Please understand, I'm trying to help here. I know all kinds of writers--good, bad (awful, even), and everything in-between. And that includes newbies as well as pros. And while everyone loves a pat on the back, as writers we must accept that some folks won't like what we write no matter how good it is. And I'm not even talking about the trolls. I'll get to them soon enough. (Writing requires great patience, so exercise some!)

I'm talking about regular, ordinary, garden variety readers. The kind who buy books every now and then, who have favorites among writers, and who frequent bookstores, libraries and on-line sources. *Those* people. Your work is going to make some of them deliriously happy. Others will respond to your

latest 500-plus page tome with a hearty "Meh." If you're lucky, you'll get more reviews out of the former. The latter usually don't care enough to offer their thoughts. Be happy about that. Indeed, be thankful!

Then there are the "legitimate" critiquers. These could be people you've asked to read over your material. They could be in your writer's group (assuming you have one; all writers need 'em whether they'll admit it or not); they could be academics, assuming you can find a college level writing program that knows anything about commercial fiction (most don't); or they could be "serious" reviewers, paid by some periodical like *Publisher's Weekly*. The point is, someone in that cadre is going to take shots at your work--maybe honestly, maybe not. Either way, they're going to hurt.

The last group to comment includes two kinds of shit slingers. First come the trolls, who post hateful reviews because they think it's funny, or because they're brain damaged, or because their mothers didn't love them enough at birth, or simply because they're off their meds. The second group is comprised of idiots. These are folks who'll give your short story collection a bad review because they don't like short stories of *any* kind. Or they'll pan your romance because they only like westerns, or because the cover illustration didn't reveal enough skin, or too much. These people will complain that your clearly labeled science fiction novel is--wait for it--science fiction! Who knew?

Someone, somewhere along the way, is going to define your work as a fresh pile of warm excrement. And when they do, you need to suck it up and keep working on your next pile. Do not even *think* about responding to a negative review. It's both pointless and self-destructive. No good can come of it. Ever!

At best you'll simply feed the troll; nobody else is likely to give it a second thought. The troll, however, will revel in his power to make you miserable. And he might even drag his little cabal of troll buddies in to help. "Good" folk will scatter for fear of being splashed. Your friends will close their eyes and pretend it didn't happen. The trolls, however, will have an orgy. Right there on your review page or website. Don't encourage them. Ignore them. Eventually they'll go away.

If you're in a critique group, just shut up. Nod your head. Thank the folks who took the time to read and respond, then go home. Have a drink. Kick the dog. Throw cold water on your parakeet. Do whatever you have to do to get the pissy feeling out of your system. Once you've cooled down and the tears have dried, take the time to consider what they said. You might find some truth there. You might find a way to save yourself from something truly embarrassing.

Then take the time to fix it. Or--and this is **always** an option--ignore 'em all and stick with what you've done.

Try this for practice:

Write your very own dreadful review. Have fun with it! Pick on your work in every possible way you can. Who knows? You might discover something you never realized before, and best of all, you'll find it before it's too late to fix!

~*~.

Chapter 33
Hey, wait--that's not an Outline!

It's usually not a good idea to generalize about writers; their sheer numbers provide an army of folks who defy the norms. While pundits and professors are busy making lists of techniques, charting dos and don'ts, and codifying creativity, the writers are busy churning out an endless stream of exceptions to the "rules." When it comes to outlines, the same things apply.

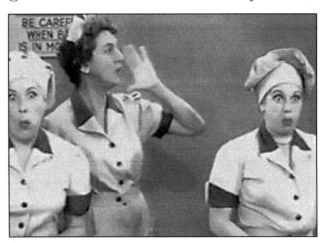

We're introduced to outlining at a tender age, and we're shown precisely how to proceed, logically cataloging ideas and expanding on them with ever-narrowing headers, sub-headers, sub-sub-headers, fonts and font sizes, Roman numerals, English letters, and Arabic numbers. Is it any wonder the only people who like doing outlines are the people who enjoy diagramming sentences? *[JL trundles off muttering, "There oughta be a law...."]*

Obviously, I'm not enamored of outlines, but I recognize they can be useful at times. When Barbara Galler-Smith and I wrote the **Druids** trilogy, for instance, we would have been hopelessly lost without the detailed outlines we maintained. And yet, when I wrote my first solo novel, ***Resurrection Blues***, I managed to plow through it with little more than a few hastily scribbled notes.

So, where's the middle ground? No two writers operate the same way (thank goodness), but we do tend to have many of the same problems. Sometimes an outline can go a long way toward solving them. Now, just because I do outlines in a particular fashion doesn't mean everyone should do the same, but at least I have a rationale for my behavior.

My approach to writing a novel these days begins in pure pantser** mode. I sit down and start typing. This usually lasts for several days during which time I'll generate a dozen scenes, give or take a couple, and I'll introduce a handful of plot lines and point of view characters. Things move swimmingly, because my

primary job is to bring players on stage and put them in jeopardy. I'm on the front end of the juggle, tossing one ball after another into the air. Somewhere about this time, the balls morph into nasty, sharp-bladed things under the authoritarian rule of gravity. They're now falling--all at once--and suddenly I notice some knave has handcuffed my hands behind my back and nailed my scuffies to the deck.

This is typically when I realize I could use a bit o' guidance, so I start an outline. I use a very simple table and record three things per scene: 1) the name of the point of view character, 2) the number of words used, and 3) what vital thing occurred. I can usually cram the latter into a single *brief* sentence. The nice thing about this approach is that I can tell at a glance who's turn it is to appear next in the story. It also helps me to evaluate whether or not what I've committed a scene to is worth the page space I've given it.

F'rinstance, if I put 500 words into a scene in which Joe wakes up and discovers someone's stolen his liver and 2,500 words into a scene where he suspects his wife is fooling around on him, I may have a case of misplaced priorities. I can also ascertain that I've left out the scene where Joe's wife agrees to let someone extract his liver in exchange for a trip to Bermuda and a pedicure.

This is also a great time to kill scenes that don't do enough. Being brutal helps.

Point is, it's quick, relatively painless, and helps me to stay focused. I've even made some outline entries *before* I've written the scenes--usually when I experience the "Ah ha!" moment which, for me, is when I realize I *can* actually finish the story I started! And yes, it's cause for celebration.

**A "pantser" is one who writes by the seat of his or her pants. This, as opposed to a "plotter," who plans ahead, at least a little bit. Plotters often know how a story will end before they begin. That's a strategy I heartily endorse, and I can show you a huge pile of unfinished stories which testify to the folly of hoping an ending will magically appear somewhere during the writing process. That said, I know many successful pantsers. They tend to be nice people despite their tragically flawed approach to the craft.

Try this for practice:

Dig out your work in progress. (Haven't got one? Okay, make something up.) Using a spreadsheet of some kind, or just a notepad, build a chart of your story. Start at the beginning and write down--scene by scene--who the point of view character is (provided there's more than one), what significant thing happens, and how many words long it is. Give yourself an extra column for adding stuff you think of later, like future plot point ideas, physical characteristics, etc.

~*~.

Chapter 34
The More Things Change? Nah.

We tend to hear (and repeat) the same things over and over, and when we do, we often bestow the status of "truth" upon them, even when they may not have earned it. Thus it is with "the more things change, the more

they stay the same." Fact is, it just ain't so. At least, not in my experience.

A good bit of the fiction I write is historical. I often work historical facts into contemporary stories, too. I do this sometimes for fun and sometimes because it gives readers a means to see what went on before in a different light. But the primary motive is that it makes me happy. But then, I'm weird. I know. I admit it. Still, history can be fun, especially if we didn't have to suffer through it.

Like many of us, I get a good deal of email that's been passed from person to person as if it were holy writ, even if the information is suspect. Snopes.com and similar sites can be helpful in verifying what's is or isn't nonsense. Sifting fact from fiction in the historical record sometimes requires more effort. But it can pay off.

A few days ago, I received an email with the following revelations, many of which I <u>was</u> (happily) able to confirm:

100 years ago:

- The average life expectancy for men in the US was 47 years.
- Fuel for the 1914 Ford Model T (and every other gas powered vehicle) was sold in drug stores and nowhere else.
- A mere 14 percent of American homes had a bathtub.
- Only 8 percent of US homes had a telephone.
- There were only 8,000 cars and only 144 miles of paved roads.
- The maximum speed limit in most cities was 10 mph.
- The tallest structure in the world was the Eiffel Tower.
- The average US wage in 1910 was 22 cents per hour.
- The average US worker made between $200 and $400 per year.

What I found fascinating about these facts is that they suggest a setting I'd never thought about. As I read over them, my mind churned up one plot possibility after another. How could I best tap into this material and create a world my

readers would enjoy? After a bit of reflection, I realized I could turn *any* of these nuggets into a story, or at least the beginning of one.

When I looked for something cool to

illustrate the second item above, I was surprised to see three diverse interpretations. Need a hint? (They're all "T" models.)

There are plenty more stats to consider, and any of these could provide fodder for an interesting tale--all from the first 15 years of the 20th century:

- A competent accountant could expect to earn $2000 per year, a dentist $2,500 per year, a veterinarian between $1,500 and $4,000 per year, and a mechanical engineer about $5,000 per year.
- More than 95 percent of all births took place at home.
- Ninety percent of all Doctors had no college education. Instead, they attended so-called "medical schools," many of which were condemned in the press and the government as "substandard."
- Sugar cost four cents a pound; coffee was fifteen. Eggs were fourteen cents a dozen.
- Most women only washed their hair once a month, and used Borax or egg yolks for shampoo. (No wonder hats were so popular!)
- Canada passed a law that prohibited poor people from entering into their country for any reason.

In 1914, about half of the US flags on display had fewer than the required 48 stars, since the flag changed with the admission of new states four times between 1896 and 1912. Here are a few more factual tidbits from that year, just in case the first batch didn't do the trick:

- The population of Las Vegas, Nevada, topped out at 30. (No kidding!)
- Crossword puzzles, canned beer, and iced tea hadn't been invented yet.
- There was neither a Mother's Day nor a Father's Day.
- One out of every five adults couldn't read or write, and only 6 percent of all Americans had graduated from high school.

- Marijuana, heroin, and morphine were all available, over the counter, at the local corner drugstore. Back then, some pharmacists claimed, "Heroin clears the complexion, gives buoyancy to the mind, regulates the stomach and bowels, and is, in fact, a perfect guardian of health!"
- Eighteen percent of households had at least one full-time servant or domestic.
- There were about 230 reported murders, per year, in the *entire* country.

Story ideas exist everywhere. You only have to expend a little effort to find more than you could possibly use.

Try this for practice:

Pick out three interesting facts from the lists presented here and write an opening for a story based on them. Make everything else up! That should be easy enough for anyone who claims to be a writer.

Go for it!

~*~

Chapter 35
Story or Joke? You Decide

"Two dinosaurs walk into a bar..."

For most of the 20th century folks believed our species evolved into something like its "modern" form around 40,000 years ago. I suspect that's about the time we started telling jokes, too.

Jokes are the simplest form of storytelling once one goes beyond, "Don't move, or that big thing with lotsa teeth will eat you," although that's not particularly funny. (Hey, I get it; not everyone can tell a joke.) Allow me to put this in question form: what differentiates a joke from a short story, usually a very short one? I suspect the answer has to do with the quality of the writing; it's certainly not just a matter of length. Can a joke have all the elements found in a story? Some can, and I just happen to have an example.

The first time I saw this story was years ago, long before the internet. In those days, office types used to find these gems, photocopy them and pass 'em around on paper. Email put an end to that, and such stories are still being forwarded at light-speed all over the planet. A couple years back, someone sent it to me. I doubt it had ever been punctuated correctly, and no one had taken the time to clean up the misspelled words, polish the dialog, or do much of anything else with it. And yet, it had all the earmarks of a complete story. See for yourself. Herewith, a well-scrubbed version of a tale I call "Coming Clean."

Poignant, isn't it?

Right. But let's take a closer look and examine this thing to see if it has all the requisite parts of a complete story. For the sake of simplicity, I'll use the 7-Point Plotting checklist to make the determination.

So, does it have a beginning which features character, setting and conflict? Indeed it does. Jonathan is in bed, and his death is imminent. We can check off the top three items: a person, in a place, with a problem.

Characters in conflict make up

Coming Clean

Jonathan lay on his deathbed, the covers tight across his chest. Rebecca, his wife of twenty years, maintained a vigil. As she had for several days, she held his hand and either wept or prayed. On this night she prayed, for he had little time left.

Her voice woke him. He looked up, and his thin, drawn lips moved ever so slightly. "Becky," he whispered.

"Hush now," she said. "Rest. Don't talk."

"Becky, there's something I... something I must tell you."

"There's no need." She brushed the hair from his forehead. "It's all right. Go back to sleep."

"No," he insisted. "I must be honest, even if it's too late to make a difference."

"Very well then, go on."

His face twisted with guilt. "I-- I slept... with your sister."

"Oh, Jon," she groaned. "I--"

"No, there's more, and I must get it off my chest." He took a deep breath then said, "I also slept with your best friend."

Rebecca shook her head. "You don't need--"

"I'm not finished," he said, looking terribly nervous. "As despicable as it is, I must confess I also slept... with your mother."

"I know," Rebecca answered softly. "That's why I poisoned you."

the heart of good fiction. A character needs a motive; he needs to act upon it, and he needs to face the consequences. In 7-Point Plotting parlance such actions and consequences are known as "Try/Fails." A character attempts to satisfy his motivation, and he either succeeds or he fails. In either case, the outcome usually leads to yet another complication. Jonathan's motive is to confess his sins, and he makes three efforts, all successful. So we can check off "Try" and "Fail."

The last two elements of the 7-Point formula call for a climax and a denouement. Old Jon's third bit of soul-scrubbing meets the criteria for a climax. It's the final attempt, the last hurrah, the grand effort, and sweet Rebecca supplies the denouement, or wrap-up, with her closing line. It's all said and done. We know who's who and what's what, and the story is over.

So, in a mere 200 words we have a complete story--beginning, middle and end. And it's funny, too. Not a bad deal.

Try this for practice:

Think of an old joke you remember from way back, preferably **way, way** back. Jot it down in raw form, then look it over in terms of 7-point plotting. Are all the elements there? If not, can you add them? If so, rewrite the joke as a short story. Embellish as needed. You're a storyteller, after all; it's what you do!

~*~

Chapter 36
Bad Words in Good Books?

I don't always use the most genteel words in my writing. But that doesn't apply to all the writing I do. If, for instance, I'm working on something destined for a family publication, or for the rare (for me) kid-targeted piece, I'll avoid "bad" words entirely.

Problem is, we don't all think of the same words as being "bad." It obviously depends on one's judgment. I'd like to think I have a pretty normal outlook on what's acceptable in mixed company and what isn't. That said, I've still used a few 4-letter gems that I later learned were not universally well received. That's too bad, because chances are, whoever felt distress hearing words like "hell"

and "damn" almost certainly missed some of the important parts of what I was saying.

And then there's the whole issue of what is or isn't "politically correct." I'm not up for that topic as it's only going to trigger a sincerely un-PC rant from me.

Somewhere in between the extremes of prissiness and political correctness lies the verbal domain I aim to occupy. That's enough elbow room for me. For others, maybe not.

Take blogger/writer Chuck Wendig for example (at **terribleminds**). He's not only a gifted writer of both fiction and non-fiction, but his blogs consistently offer terrific advice and counsel on the writing craft and the publishing industry. There's no question he knows what he's talking about. HOWEVER [drum roll] he constantly carpet bombs his blogs with profanity. I suspect he's doing it for shock value, but when the bomb bay doors are open that wide, the result is more like "schlock" value. That's a shame, because he's got so much great stuff buried in there. Alas, *my* readership tends to be a tad older and predominantly middle-class, so I don't often recommend his blog posts because I know the F-bombs, in particular, will prevent many of them from seeing the really valuable information he has to share.

Geez. So now *I'm* part of the PC police? Say it ain't so!

More important than how I regard naughty words is how *you* deal with them. Do you know your target audience well enough to determine what sorts of words you can get away with? We've all been to enough movies lately where the F-word seems to be the primary adjective and verb. And in some, I swear (pardon the pun), it's the **only** adjective. That doesn't strike me as terribly imaginative. After you've heard the word eight hundred times, the autonomic filters go up, and it becomes nothing more than background noise.

I've used the F-word in several of my books, but I don't make a habit of it. I save it for shock value. That may sound odd in this day and age, but if my characters don't talk that way day-to-day, readers will definitely know something's up when they do start using that sort of language.

What you do with so-called "bad" language is up to you. If you're going to use it, I suggest you use it for a reason, not because it's handy. Figure out how to get some mileage from it. If it comes from the mouth of a child, for instance, provide readers with an explanation of how that happened. Little people, big ears. We've all seen it happen. In your book, you'll need to make it real. And hopefully, funny.

I recall reading Steven Pressfield's **Gates of Fire**, a monster bestseller about the battle of Thermopylae. In it he provides page after page of dialog from the mouths of Spartan heroes. Yet, the dialog seemed to have come straight from a modern army barracks, complete with drill sergeants whose vocabularies consisted entirely of four-letter words. Profanity isn't new, by any means, and I'm sure Pressfield's intent was to capture the "feel" of men readying themselves for combat. But from a purely historical perspective, I'm sure there's no way in hell those guys talked like that.

When my great friend, Barb Galler-Smith, and I were working on the **Druids** trilogy, which is set in the 1st century BC--considerably *later* than the Pressfield story--we went out of our way to find out just how warriors of that era swore. What was considered profane? The answer surprised us, but upon reflection, it made sense. Expressions such as "God's blood" or "Scathach's abode" might not carry the gutter **gravitas** of contemporary curses, but even Anglicized as these are, they were more faithful to the period. We were fine with that, as were our readers.

The upshot? Use good judgment, even if it hurteth.

~*~.

Chapter 37
You're Stuck? There's a Fix

Where did it all go wrong? Your story was cooking along nicely right up until-- Hm. Somehow, somewhere along the way, something happened--either to the plot or your enthusiasm. Maybe both. Or maybe it was something else, some wrong turn, loose end, or forgotten clue. Now it's sitting forlorn and half-finished, give or take a few thousand words, with a formerly proud parent in hand-wringing mode trying to decide how best to achieve some kind of consolation. [Hint: bourbon works, but it's only temporary, and it won't do anything to get the story back on track.]

Just knowing you aren't the first to slide into this sad state doesn't help much. Nor does the knowledge that the universe is awash in unfinished, trunked, junked or klunked manuscripts. Back burners from Beantown to Bora Bora are crowded with stories that started out great then turned into whimpering piles of literary slag, or snot, or worse. But, before you work your way through all the supposed stages of grief--probably somewhere between depression and acceptance (but after denial, anger and bargaining)--understand that there might be hope.

More than likely, the problem lies in one of three areas: a plot problem--be it primary or secondary; a major lack of conflict; or your characters aren't pulling their weight. Naturally, each of these groupings has a variety of constituent issues. We'll tackle 'em all in this chapter. Have tissues handy.

Without reading what you've done so far it's impossible to diagnose specific plot problems. What I *can* discuss are issues commonly associated with plot problems. The first of these is boredom. Your plot simply doesn't hold your attention. It probably did when you started, but now? Meh. Not so much.

Why? And more importantly, what to do?

1) You could start by dreaming up a subplot. Find something that'll shake up your characters and give one or more of them something to worry about. Even if your subplot unwinds quickly, it'll shift attention away from your sagging primary plot. If it's more involved, it could amplify the main storyline.

Subplots needn't be complex. They can start with something as simple as an odd turn, an unexpected shift in attitude, or a mystery--something that just doesn't seem to make sense. Nor are you limited in the <u>number</u> of subplots you concoct. As long as you have a decent stable of characters to link them to, you can dream up as many subplots as you can keep track of.

2) There's a good chance you have no bloody idea where your story is going. (Listen up, pantsers!) You've got at least three options:

A- Find the plot holes now, and fix 'em. You probably know where they are, or at the very least, you've got suspicions about where they are. Take the time now to identify them and figure out how you're going to plug them.

B- Outline your opus, even if you had an outline to begin with, because obviously, it ain't working. Go back and outline it again--start to finish--based on what you've written, not on what you **intended** to write before you got sidetracked, your car died, or your dear aunt Sue married the abominable snowman/used car salesman. Use whatever outline format works for you, from the most detailed to the least. Just do it!

C- If the thought of outlining is more than you can bear, do at least one thing: **_figure out how your story ends_**. Nail it down--who lives, who doesn't, everything. *Write* it down, too. Don't mess around with this, it's critical.

Assuming your plot works, and you have enough subplots to carry the load when your primary storyline begins to buckle, you might still be road blocked by character issues. You wouldn't be the first writer to discover your protagonist isn't everything you thought she was. There's a good chance you've found and fallen in love with one or more shiny new characters who do nifty things, get involved in deep mysteries, have passionate sex, or otherwise wrestle around in the **Do Stuff** portion of your hindbrain.

It's time to trot those rascals out! Turn them into Point Of View players. Very often a different look at the same old problems--especially if skewed by an oddball perspective--will make the old stuff new again. Or at least more palatable.

The logical alternative to having your characters do things, is to invent nasty things you can do to them. [Cue: dark, evil laughter] Seriously, readers care more about how characters persevere than they do about how they look, what they say, or where they come from. The more dastardly the tricks you play, the more dear those players become in your reader's mind.

Let's reflect a moment on what makes a plot twist diabolical. In a perfect world, you'll be introducing a threat which operates on two or more levels.

Physical threats are the easiest: "Give up the secret, or we'll cut your leg off." Physical threats with an **emotional** component are a little harder, but just as effective: "Give up the secret, or we'll cut your kid's leg off." Figuring out how to work in a ~~philosophical~~ threat is likely the hardest of all, but it, too, can be devastating: "Give up the secret, or we'll cut your kid's leg off <u>and</u> make everyone think you did it." *Psychological (typo per Josh)

There are a host of fairly common ways to launch your character(s) in different directions. None of these is particularly fresh and new, but they've all been well received by readers, so you'll be on fairly safe ground to use them:

- Introduce someone with a dark and dreadful secret.

- Arrange for an unexpected sexual tryst between two (three?) main players.
- Bring in a new character so strange he/she upsets everyone and everything.
- Kill off a character unexpectedly. Use a level of gruesomeness to fit your story.
- Have someone betray your protagonist.

As an alternative, you can always do the "What If" dance. This involves asking a dozen "what if" questions about your plot(s). Record the answers. Write 'em all down. Don't cheat! This is a great time to get crazy. No idea is too weird or too funky. No character is off-limits; no mayhem is too great, no sin too unthinkable.

This is bold, blue sky stuff--free range, get naked, don't even *think* about staying inside the box kinda material. Kill, maim, coerce, rape, strangle, lie, molest, badger, blackmail, bonesaw and/or banish any player who hasn't been toting his own weight. Be cruel, quick, and decisive. Then step back and see what yumminess you've wrought. At this point you're free to change anything and everything, right? If not, you wouldn't have gotten stuck in the first place! Put it all on the table--everything--every last bit of whatever you've got.

Because the alternative means giving up, throwing yet another story into the trunk and never looking at it again.

And if none of that works, take a meat cleaver to the last 5 or 10 thousand words you've written. Obviously, they've led you astray. They're not working; so nuke 'em, and good riddance. (Yes, of course I know it'll hurt like hell, but you'll be better off without 'em. And besides, we both know you're going to copy them to another file just in case you want to get 'em back. I can *almost* guarantee you won't want them later on, but that's another discussion.)

Finally, we come to the ultimate approach, the last resort, the final directive. Oddly, this works for an astonishing number of writers, especially those who've examined all the foregoing alternatives and found them totally unacceptable. Maybe it's time to just grit your teeth and keep on keepin' on. Write your way outta the fog. There's a perfectly palatable answer in there somewhere. You've just got to dig it out.

If that doesn't work, open your wallet, make sure it contains lots and lots of spendable cash, and pay me to figure it out for you. I'll be more than happy to take a look. My rates are semi-negotiable ("semi'" meaning somewhere between expensive and exorbitant), but I guarantee results. I won't guarantee you'll like 'em. I will promise, however, to point out a way to the finish line. You'll still have to make the journey.

(Wow, long chapter. And now you're probably wondering how in the world I'd come up with an exercise that fits this topic. I mean, c'mon--we all get stuck from time to time, right? Well, as you might have guessed, I got stuck for an exercise. So, just relax and be thankful!)

~*~

Chapter 38
Are We There Yet?

Quite a few of the writers I know have a tendency to edit their work beyond death and well into the hereafter. There's certainly no shame in wanting your work to be as good as you can make it. That's a tremendously noble goal, and one I wish every writer aimed to achieve. But at some point you have to step away from it, admit you've been changing the same sentences over and over again, and let the damn thing crawl outta the nest!

I imagine most of this hesitation to release a fledgling is based on inexperience. This could be a first novel, a cherished short story, or a particularly poignant memoir. It must be important to you or you wouldn't have labored over it so long and hard. But it's more than likely among the earliest of your efforts. You want it perfect. You don't want anyone to see it until you've smoothed out every sentence, agonized over every syllable of dialog, tweaked and twiddled every possible nuance.

The thing is, until you've written a couple million words (give or take a few hundred thousand), you likely aren't skilled enough to recognize what ought to

be tweaked and twiddled, and what ought to be left the hell alone! And that's perfectly okay--you're a newbie after all. How could you know **everything**? I've been at this stuff for decades, and I sure don't know all there is to know about it. Far from it. But thankfully, I have picked up a few things here and there.

Do the best work you're capable of, and try not to expect more of yourself than any reasonable person would. Then set the work aside for a while--maybe a couple weeks or even longer; a month or two wouldn't hurt--then coax it from its cage and read it out loud, with feeling. **Every. Single. Word.** And do it in a dramatic fashion, as if you had an audience of film makers who want to *experience* each of those nuances over which you labored so diligently. What you'll discover is that most of it is pretty darned good. It works. It resonates. Yes, there are spots that are a little thin, but if you take the time to highlight 'em while you're reading it'll be a simple matter to go back and address them.

Then it's on to your First Readers. I put the title in caps because what they do is so important. They'll find the nits and wrinkles that you--the writer--just can't see. Provided you have a good rapport with them, the feedback you get will be priceless. They will make it possible for you to walk your baby right out the door into the big, scary world.

The trick is to find *good* First Readers. In most cases, these are <u>not</u> people you live with or to whom you're related. They aren't folks you work with unless you're of the same rank. Subordinates and superiors should always be left out of the mix. You need people who know at least a little something about writing. And, they need to know you're more interested in the truth than you are in having them make you feel good. Get that nonsense out of the way NOW!

Then read the feedback, make the changes YOU think are reasonable, and mark the work "done." Take your significant other or best pal out for dinner or ice cream, or whatever is most appropriate, and celebrate your success. You're finished! It's *done!*

But in retrospect, maybe I've got this all wrong. I'd better take another look at it in the morning.

SageOfTheSouth.wordpress.com

And now it's time to go back to the other project you started while this one cooled off. Rinse and repeat. Write and succeed.

Try this for practice:

Okay, this isn't really writing practice; it's an exercise to help you get ready to let your baby go. Make a list of people you can ask to read and review your work. Make sure they know something about writing, and make sure they understand you want truth, not flattery, and that you're willing to compensate them for their time, somehow, even if it means babysitting for their kids.

~*~.

Chapter 39
Enough with the Dots Already!

Someone asked me recently why I wasn't on Twitter. I almost said, "because I'm

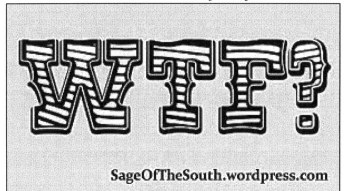

SageOfTheSouth.wordpress.com

already on bourbon." But then I thought that would be a little too snarky, even if it was true. The real reason is more basic. Based on the admittedly limited number of tweets I've seen, it's obvious no one using that medium bothers with grammar, or spelling, or punctuation. Reading tweets is like attending a convention of e e cummings wannabes.

The thing to remember about the late Mr. Cummings (1894-1962), is that he learned the rules, and actually used them for years, before he opted to ignore them. He wrote reams and reams of stuff (mostly poetry, but also plays and novels) arranged and punctuated in accordance with the syntax of traditional English. He wasn't screwing around with the language; that's a more recent phenomenon.

Twitter, along with its grammatically evil counterpart--the dreaded *txt msg*-- have taken our language into a bad place, one devoid of anything save expediency. And one of the worst of its sins is the substitution of dots for virtually any punctuation mark. I'm not even talking about ellipsis, the three dots which indicate either missing words or a bit of dialog which trails off. I'm talking about a random sprinkling of dots--two, five, forty-one--however many the twit (twiterer?) or text jockey chooses to use.

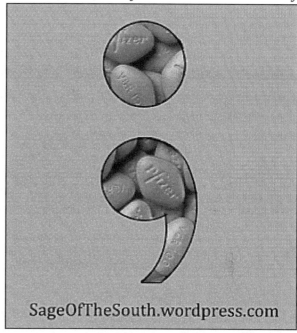

SageOfTheSouth.wordpress.com

- dude...... you goin r not
- beer nite.. be ther bro
- car dead can u gimme ride

Do I fear for the future? Indeed. [sigh]

I used to be content ranting about the misuse of semicolons. The poor things have been wedged into more manuscripts than clowns into cars at the circus. And with about as much usefulness. Listen up: Semi-colons are <u>not</u> commas on steroids; they aren't typographically **aroused**, and they certainly don't provide a magical answer to any and all grammatical conundrums. What they do is connect two sets of words which could otherwise stand alone quite nicely as complete sentences.

Da rule is:
"i" before "e" except
after a semi-colon.

SageOfTheSouth.wordpress.com

Why do that? Well, mostly to show a cause and effect relationship. F'rinstance: "Bob's stomach grumbled; he went to find food." There are only two other ways to do this: break 'em into separate sentences, or connect them with a comma and a coordinating conjunction, (like: and, or, but, so, etc.) So, "Bob's stomach grumbled**, and** he went to find food."

One can also use the noble semi-colon to separate complete clauses in a list:

137

"Wanda had high cheekbones; she had the legs of a dancer; she had the manners of a hyena in heat." (Actually, I know Wanda, and she's really a sweet gal. A little crazy at times, but hey, aren't we all?)

An editor of one of a premier speculative fiction magazine once told me she loved to see the proper use of a semi-colon in the opening of a story because it demonstrated the writer's knowledge of that much grammar at least. If the same, crummy little punctuation mark was **misused**, it told her to be wary of the writer's work. Would you trust a builder who didn't know how to use his tools?

The point is, like so many elements of the craft, you should learn the rules before breaking them so that when you **do** break 'em, you'll be doing it for a good reason and not because you're some kind of knuckle-dragging troglodyte.

Please, don't let anyone think you're a troglodyte. Even Wanda.

Try this for practice:

Dig up your work in progress and scan the whole thing for semi-colons (there's a "Find" feature in every decent word processor). Examine each one to be sure you haven't screwed it up. The preceding page gives a splendid explanation of the role of the semi-colon.

Next, do the same for any random sprinkling of dots.

Fuss at me now, but later, when editors see what you've done, they'll think you're a genius!

Chapter 40
How Long Should a Story Be?

It depends. Although the question isn't nearly as stupid as, say, "How tall is a battleship. True or False?"

In traditional publishing, manuscript length has some generally agreed upon standards. The most common of these are: short story, novelette, novella and novel. One could also add a couple more categories fore and aft: flash fiction and epic. For convenience sake, here's a general guide:

- Flash fiction: 25-1,000 words
- Short story: 500-10,000 words
- Novelette: 7,500-20,000 words
- Novella: 20,000-50,000 words
- Novel: 50,000-120,000 words
- Epic: over 120,000 words

You'll notice there's some overlap. And, to be completely honest, the "limits" are fuzzy and vary by publisher. According to Wikipedia, the longest novel in a single volume (in English) is Samuel

Richardson's ***Clarissa, or, the History of a Young Lady***, first published in 1748. Penguin Classics produced a 1,534-page paperback version in 1986. It has an estimated word length of just under a million. (I haven't read it, but I suspect Clarissa was a *very* busy girl.)

When it comes to per word rates, flash fiction probably has the highest potential, especially since so-called "Pro" rates for short fiction are still under ten cents a word.

Short stories over 5K in length continue to be a tough sell, and God help you if you're trying to sell something in the novelette range. They're generally far too long for most magazines and far too short for traditional book publishers. If you're lucky enough to have two or three of them handy, you could bundle them. Your best bet for this length is in ebooks. Many readers are looking for something they can zip through during a commute or two. If you self-publish, be sure your work is listed in the proper genre. Commuters can be a finicky lot. But they can also be loyal. Write good stuff, and they'll come back for more.

Most writers I know have their sights set on writing novels. From my experience, the "desired" length for traditional publishers is in the 90-110K range. These make for great mass market paperbacks. The spines are big enough to see on a shelf, and yet they don't take up *too* much space. They also command decent prices--all things which will warm a Harvard MBA's heart (assuming they still have one; a fact not in evidence).

Full disclosure: my nephew is a Harvard MBA, but he's not in the publishing biz, and I'm fairly certain he doesn't follow my blog. And kindly don't ask if he's read my revolutionary war novel (***Treason, Treason!***) which should have been on his list of all-time faves. 'Course, he has to read the damn thing first.

Anyway, there you have it. I'm guessing that unless you're a world class, bestselling author, you probably oughta stick to lengths under a million words. Way under.

Companion question: how long is a chapter? Or a scene?

As long as it needs to be. I shoot for about 4K words per chapter, which I think is about the right amount to keep someone awake who's reading in bed. Scene length? For me, the minimum is one sentence, more or less. Max? 4K, give or take, just like a chapter. Doncha just love coincidence?

In the long run, I don't think chapter and/or scene length is important. Pace, however, is critical. If your scene lacks the proper pace, it won't matter how long it is. We'll take a look at that in the next chapter.

Yes, by God, you will take five cents a word!

Try this for practice:

Finish a story! Count the words (or, if you're smart, let your word processor do it for you), then use the handy chart to determine how tough it'll be to market.

~*~.

Chapter 41
It's About Pacing, Not Walking

Have you ever picked up a book, tuned in to a TV show, or sat down to watch a movie and found yourself bored or disappointed because nothing happened? For a novice writer, or one with a limited number of fiction sales, that's the *last* thing you want a reader to think while looking at your stuff.

And yet, it happens. Often. And the reasons are fairly common. In my experience the two most likely causes are a writer who falls in love with his own words, or a writer who doesn't take the time to match the pace of his writing to the pace of his story. Fortunately, both conditions can be corrected, but the cure requires the writer to set aside ego and surrender to practicality.

Most budding writers tend to over-write but under-edit. This results in work that's either too complex--"purple prose"--or laden with weasel words, saidbooks and unneeded speech tags. And that only covers the **opening** (arguably the most important part of any story).

Pacing also applies to story arc, the rise and fall of tension within the overall work. We'll restrict our study to "local" pacing here and start with a sample story opening, that hasn't been edited (enough):

Like an army of invisible barbarians, the wind struck the house one gust after another. The repeated attacks against the weakening structure came with the *sounds* of warfare, too. The groans from the building mimicked those of the dying on a battlefield, and while the ancient, weather-grayed farmhouse shuddered from the assault, it seemed unwilling to surrender, unwilling to give in to the inevitable demands of nature, unable to rest from the ongoing struggle to remain upright.

Inside, another battle raged as Jett Fordham fought to keep a fire going. The hearth was old, the chimney built of fieldstone. On balance it lacked as much mortar between the rocks as it maintained. The updraft remained weak, and smoke from the miserable excuse for a blaze grew thicker within the room. Jett's options seemed to be limited to death by exposure or death from smoke inhalation.

While I readily admit to a lack of credentials when it comes to scene-setting, I feel confident in spotting one that's overdone. My first editing impulse would be to nuke the entire first paragraph and focus on poor Jett, shivering inside a ramshackle house trying to light a damp log with a pack of old matches. However, I  recognize that a certain amount of scene-setting helps set the tone, too. So I'd settle for putting graf one on a diet and reducing it to:

Like an army of invisible barbarians, the wind struck the house one gust after another. The groans from the building mimicked those of the dying on a battlefield, and while the ancient, weather-grayed farmhouse shuddered from the assault, it <u>wouldn't</u> surrender. (Added word underscored.)

That much of it I could live with, although the warfare analogy is still a bit overworked. The second graf is closer to actual story material, but some streamlining wouldn't hurt. To wit:

Inside, Jett Fordham fought to keep a fire going. The hearth was old, the chimney built of <u>badly mortared</u> fieldstone. The updraft remained weak, and smoke grew thick within the room. Jett's options seemed limited to death by exposure or death from smoke inhalation.

The objective here is not to eliminate "luxurious" prose; the goal is to improve the pace. If this story were intended for a literary magazine, I'd be tempted to leave some of the darker purple bits in. For a popfic market, however, I'd press the accelerator and leave the fluffy stuff in storage.

Let's look at a less literary attempt.

Hey there, Chuckie boy!

Jamie knew that Chuck, his best friend since forever--grade school at least, but maybe earlier than that-- was in deep, deep trouble. Chuck didn't exactly have a first-class mind, but he was a pretty decent guy nonetheless. He cared a lot for his friends, his dog, and his family. He was never intentionally mean or dishonest. The problem was, Chuck had a hard time figuring out just who his real friends were. He was simply too nice to understand that just

because someone smiled at him, that didn't make them pals. And now one of those not-exactly-a-friend types wanted him to re-pay a loan with way more interest than principal.

This passage has a certain colloquial "voice," and it's really not all that bad. But let's see what happens when the weasel words and backstory are pulled out. Watch the pace speed up as sentences get shorter and more to the point.

Jamie knew that Chuck, his best--<u>if not his brightest</u>--friend, was in deep trouble. Chuck was a decent guy<u>, but he</u> had a hard time figuring out who his real friends were<u>, and</u> now one of those not-a-friend types wanted him to pay <u>off</u> a loan with <u>far</u> more interest than principal.

There's no shame in writing tight prose. In fact, I'd argue it's much easier to sell. Yes, there are markets for work which features style over substance, but they're pretty rare. If you want to sell your work, the best approach for those who haven't already established themselves, is to be direct, concise and to the point. It helps to have a damned good story, too.

Try this for practice:

Dig through your failed stories. You know the ones--they started okay, maybe even great, but then got bogged down somewhere and you lost interest. Yeah, *those* stories. Take a look at the openings of each of them with an eye to eliminating anything that didn't contribute something of value. Whack out the weasel words, the empty phrases, and anything even remotely clichéd.

It shouldn't be too hard, especially since you've already given up on them as potentially "finish-able." But, who knows, once you've polished the openings, you might change your mind.

~*~

Chapter 42
In Closing: 10 Things to Avoid

Congratulations--you've not only managed to work your way through this book, you've finished a story, too!. You'd be amazed at how many people can't say that. Fortunately, you're not one of them. So, what do you *do* with that finished story?

Even though you're eager to send it out, I beg you to take a look at this list first and make sure you don't do anything on it. That's for your benefit, not mine. And as a reward, I'll give you the name and web address of a fantastic site which lists all kinds of valuable data about possible markets for your work.

Clichés Suck

But first, the list--in no particular order:

1) Do NOT open your story with a cliché. "It was a dark and stormy night" might work for Snoopy (or Edward Bulwer-Lytton who first penned it in 1830), but everyone else should avoid it like a communicable disease.

2) Never start your tale with a truly interesting character, and then reveal that this player has no real role in your story. He, or she, is merely a spear carrier, and the **real** story begins somewhere else.

3) Beginning a novel with a dream sequence is all but guaranteed to land your manuscript in the reject bin. If you must use dreams, use them later, and let the reader know.

4) Editors who read short stories typically have an aversion to any story which begins with a protagonist in a plain white room. Anyone who's ever sat at a computer or in front of a typewriter knows what a blank screen or an empty page looks like. Keep groping, please.

5) Don't start with a description of the weather. Nobody cares. Weather is boring, even really, really dreadful weather. B-O-R-I-N-G. And the reason it's boring is because it's been done to death.

6) Efforts to get chummy with the reader will NOT be rewarded. Phrases such as "dear reader" or "gentle reader" went out with gas lights and spats. Use one, and your manuscript will go that way, too.

7) Try not to kill off your protagonist at the end of scene (or chapter) one. Editors, like most readers, will wonder why they wasted their time.

8) Don't employ something outlandish that has nothing to do with your story in order to stimulate interest. A graphic encounter between your super-spy, a prostitute from the planet Gorgon, and a pair of rabid chinchillas will *not* ensure that anyone will read further.

9) Never submit a sloppy manuscript. This means you must clean up misspelled words, bad grammar, and poor

composition before you send your work out into the world. If you can't take the time to learn how to correct these things, consider hiring a copyeditor to do it for you. If you plan to write more than one book, this will become an ever-increasing and more time-consuming expense. It makes more sense to simply learn the craft.

10) Always address your cover letter to a real person, by name and title. You're asking them to do you the courtesy of reading your manuscript. The least you can do is pay them the courtesy of learning their name.

So, now that we're all clear on that, here's the website address I promised:

http://www.ralan.com

I've used Ralan's listings for years, and he's never steered me wrong.

(Another awkward, don't-have-an-exercise moment. Hey, it happens. Luckily, there's something you can try in the **Appendix**. Why not give the **Simile and Metaphor Exercise** a shot. What could it hurt? Go on now, I'll wait.)

~*~

APPENDIX

The following pages contain additional information, examples of writing exercises, and challenges. It was too good to leave out, but too involved to work into existing chapters. Some of the writing work required is easy, and some of it is hard, kinda like driving conditions in most urban environments.

Just do the best you can, and if possible, have some fun, too!

~*~

Basic Desires Theory

After conducting studies that involved more than 6,000 people, Professor Steven Reiss of Ohio State University came up with these 16 basic desires:

1) Acceptance, the need to be appreciated

2) Curiosity, the need to gain knowledge

3) Eating, the need for food

4) Family, the need to take care of one's offspring

5) Honor, the need to be faithful to the customary values of an individual's ethnic group, family or clan

6) Idealism, the need for social justice

7) Independence, the need to be distinct and self-reliant

8) Order, the need for prepared, established, and conventional environments

9) Physical activity, the need for work out of the body

10) Power, the need for control of will

11) Romance, the need for mating or sex

12) Saving, the need to accumulate something

13) Social contact, the need for relationship with others

14) Social status, the need for social significance

15) Tranquility, the need to be secure and protected

16) Vengeance, the need to strike back against another person

~*~

Josh Langston

Cliché Exercise

The following contains too many clichés to count. As you read through the paragraphs, underline all the tired, worn-out, hackneyed phrases.

In this day and age, good teachers are few and far between. My deepest, darkest secret is my desire to be one of those teachers--one that is worth his weight in gold, who works his fingers to the bone, hand in hand with students to prepare them to meet the trials and tribulations of life. With an attitude like that, my first day of teaching was doomed to disappointment. I was walking on air as I arrived at my first class, until I realized I'd forgotten my key. A wave of optimism washed over me when I saw the classroom door open. I sauntered up to the door, when BANG, like a bolt from the blue, one of my new students--later proven to be rotten to the core--darted out and slammed the door right in my face.

My anxiety was growing by leaps and bounds, when, as luck would have it, a custodian came by and unlocked the door for me. I could sense the undercurrent of excitement as I walked into the room, and the mischievous student beat a hasty retreat to her seat. Anxious for my reaction, she breathed a sigh of relief when I decided not to make a tempest in a teapot about the incident. Cool as a cucumber, I posed the first discussion prompt, "The writing process is neither writing nor a process. Discuss."

In their desire to please me, all the students jumped on the bandwagon to discuss. Slowly but surely, the humiliating experience became water under the bridge as I continue the uphill battle to become all that I can be as an instructor.

Yes, it's awful, and once you remove all the clichés, there's almost nothing left. Here's your chance to rewrite it--free of claptrap!

~*~

152

Descriptive Writing Challenge

Write a descriptive paragraph or two about each of these settings. Do your best to adhere to the restrictions, but above all, _never_ say where you are.

You're in a pet store. Do NOT mention any animal.

You're in an automotive garage. Do NOT mention cars or car repairs.

You're attending a professional wrestling match. Do NOT mention wrestlers or wrestling moves.

You're attending a rodeo. Do NOT mention cowboys or any rodeo events.

You're stuck in the Emergency Room at a hospital. Do NOT mention medical staff or patients.

You're attending a hog calling contest. Do NOT mention any members of the pig family (two- _or_ four-legged).

You're in the engine compartment of a steam locomotive. Do NOT mention trains or railroad employees.

You're in a nuclear powered submarine. Do NOT mention ships, sailors or any of the armed forces.

You're sitting in on a meeting of the UN General Assembly. Do NOT mention diplomats, statesmen or politics.

You're attending a marriage ceremony. Do NOT mention any member of the wedding party.

You're in the main branch of the New York Public Library. Do NOT mention books or shelves.

You're in a TV studio. Do NOT mention cameras, performers or production staff.

~*~

Point of View Challenge

The concierge arranged for her to meet the one locals simply called "Voodoo Man." If he had another name, no one used it. Her meeting with him went smoothly, if mysteriously. She got the potion she needed and took the first opportunity she had to administer it. The result? She would know soon.

She'd surprised herself by going through with it since the whole trip sprang from an angry decision. Her longtime paramour, a male whose name she couldn't even say without becoming emotional, had finally given her the ultimate brush off. She could never forgive him.

I should be grateful, she thought. His betrayal meant liberation. No more courting the skinny-legged ingrate; no more waiting in the wings for him to saunter off-stage; no more playing second fiddle to the fickle little fart. She'd had enough. More than enough. And to prove it, she'd traveled to this remote tropical island and its luxury resort.

The paparazzi spotted her leaving her Manhattan apartment, but her studio-supplied driver outwitted them. She boarded the plane wearing a disguise and kept it on until she reached the safety of her room. She had no choice. Her trademark platinum blonde hair, sequined gowns, and abundant *décolletage* meant instant recognition wherever she went--the downside of an adoring public.

Still, she had to escape, if only to regain her composure. Alas, her plans dissolved the moment she spotted *him*. Although he also traveled in disguise, she recognized him instantly. He sat across the first class aisle from her, but paid her no mind. That hurt. She had nursed a desire to romance the stunningly handsome Australian since she'd first seen him on screen as "Wolverine," a role he reprised often, in addition to appearing as Jean Valjean in *Les Mis.* He'd played a leading man more times than she could count.

She'd spoken to him, but he ignored her like everyone else and slept through the flight. The cabin crew hadn't recognized her, and she chose not to expose herself. Instead, she devised a new plan, one that required the services of someone exactly like "Voodoo Man." The love potion became hers just as easily; slipping it into his drink had been child's play, and now *le gran moment* was at hand.

She waltzed toward his table and seated herself opposite him in a darkened corner of the resort's most exclusive cabaret. Slipping the hood of her silken cape behind her head, she exposed the flowing silver locks which had brought her so much fame.

"It's you!" he cried, his hand atremble as he lowered his love potion-laden wine glass to the table. A look of unbridled desire on his face, the Hollywood idol reached across the table to touch her. She shifted away. It wouldn't do to let him succeed too easily.

"Have you ordered yet?" she asked.

What did it matter, he wondered. Why would she care?

"I thought we might take a walk on the beach," she said. "The sun's already set, and the moonlight on the water beckons."

"As it does to me," he said in a whisper as if his throat had suddenly gone dry. "I'd like that."

She thought briefly about taking a sip of his wine--in for a penny, in for a pound, she thought. But it was too risky, and for once she resisted temptation.

He stood abruptly. "Come," he said. "Come with me, Pi--"

"Shhhh!" She touched his lips to silence him. "Don't give me away."

She slipped her silk hood back in place and bid him to follow her to the nearby beach. Deserted now, it stretched away into darkness. He followed her like a man in a trance. Which, she realized, described him perfectly.

They had barely escaped the lights of the secluded dining spot when he took her in his arms, and they dropped to the still-warm sand of a soft dune.

Josh Langston

"I need you," he moaned, running his hands over her silk-shrouded shoulders. He couldn't explain his extraordinary desire. He had known a vast array of females, and yet this one held him utterly captive. He could think of nothing save his need and her proximity. The flimsy cape slipped away easily, her silver hair fell free in a wave of lust crashing upon the shore of her bosom.

Hugh gasped, his hands eager, searching, driven.

"Oh," she cried. "Oh. Oh. Oh!"

The bodice of her sequined gown parted, and he launched himself upon her, his desire pushing everything from his mind but her body.

And then he stopped, utterly confounded.

"My God," he moaned, "you've got--"

"What?" she asked, her own desire enflamed by his. "Touch me! You know you want to!"

"But-- But-- You have--"

"I'm yours," she implored him. "Don't stop now!"

"But... There are too many!"

"Nonsense. They're all yours--all of them!" she groaned.

And suddenly the spell vanished. Hugh Jackman staggered to his feet and backed away from the disheveled Miss Piggy, his mind reeling. He'd never experienced such confusion. "I'm sorry," he said. "I-- I just can't handle ten nipples all at once."

The words scorched her soul. Kermit had said the exact same thing.

~End~

Dialog Punctuation--by Example

The rules for punctuating dialog are pretty simple:

--Use quotation marks at the start and end of whatever a character says, and put all punctuation *inside* them**, even quoted dialog.

> **"Holy moly, Batman--look at that car!"**
> **"What car?" asked the caped crusader, ignoring his companion. "I--"**
> **"That one!" Robin screamed, shouldering him aside. "It's Bat-babe! She almost ran you down."**
> **"--huh? No. I can't believe it." Batman adjusted his new mask; he hadn't been able to see clearly since he got it. "I'm a public servant, and according to the *Almost Daily Beagle*, 'a darned good one.'"**

--Don't use quotation marks for thoughts. If a character is *thinking* (musing, considering, evaluating, etc.) put those words in italics, or use a tag to indicate it's someone's thoughts.

> **Oh, what I'd give for a chocolate sundae right now, Homer thought.**
> **Somebody mentioned chocolate sundaes, and Homer palmed his face. *Oh, yummmm!***
> **Homer paused. *I'd kill for a chocolate sundae right about now*. Instead, he got coffee.**

--Use speech and action tags *appropriately*. Match the tag to the action.

> Wrong: **"I love you," he screamed.**
> Not wrong, but not great: **"I love you," he moaned.**
> Not great, but better: **"I love you," he said, breathlessly.**
> Better still: **He embraced her and said, "I love you."**
> Best: **"I love you," he said as he revealed a 10-carat diamond engagement ring.**

--Every speaker deserves a paragraph of his own.

This is just wrong:

> "John!" "Mary!" "Come away with me," he pleaded. "I can't. The children--" "Leave 'em. They're all ingrates anyway." "You can't be serious, John! They're my *children*, for God's sake." "Wake up, Mary--they're old enough to collect Social Security!"

(Besides, it looks more appealing spread out:)

> "John!"
> "Mary!"
> "Come away with me," he pleaded.
> "I can't. The children--"
> "Leave 'em. They're all ingrates anyway."
> "You can't be serious, John! They're my *children*, for God's sake."
> "Wake up, Mary--they're old enough to collect Social Security!"

**These examples are based on commonly accepted punctuation of *American* style English. In the UK, and some of the other former colonies, they follow a different set of rules. But then, many of them drive on the wrong side of the road, too. (Canadians, God bless 'em, can't make up their minds.)

Time and Place Challenge

Revise the following two paragraphs based on the time, place and circumstances given to you. Examine the underlined words and phrases, and be sure to update all of them to make sense in light of the alternative setting assigned. Make your work colorful. You want to draw readers into the story.

Duncan drove a <u>small car</u> down the <u>dark street</u> and parked in front of a <u>big house</u>. An emotional guy, Duncan was clearly <u>agitated</u>. The <u>phone call</u> that caused him to make this trip had come unexpectedly. There had been no time to plan, let alone procure a <u>weapon</u> for what he knew was coming.

It wouldn't be long before he faced the <u>person</u> who'd <u>made his life a living hell</u>. He exited the <u>car</u>, walked to the <u>trunk</u>, and stopped. He'd stowed his <u>carpentry</u> gear in there. Maybe he didn't need a <u>gun</u> after all. Maybe he could use a <u>hammer</u>.

Where and when: **Chicago, late 1920's, Al Capone's neighborhood**

Where and when: **Acapulco, during a peasant revolt, fall of 2050**

Where and when: **London, the middle ages, during a plague**

Where and when: **San Francisco, 1906, a day after the great quake**

Where and when: **Suburban Tokyo, spring of 1944**

Where and when: **Moscow, winter of 1917**

Where and when: **Washington, DC, spring of 1862**

Where and when: **Luna City, a moon colony, 2090**

Where and when: **Dallas, 1963, the day JFK died**

Where and when: **Rome, 44BC, the day Caesar died**

Where and when: **Pompey, in the hours just before Vesuvius erupted**

~*~

Josh Langston

Simile and Metaphor Exercise

Finish the phrases with whatever metaphor or simile comes readily to mind. *To get the most from the exercise, <u>don't worry about coming up with something good, just write.</u> The idea is to get your subconscious to make connections in a new, more creative way.*

1- Blue paint spilled on the road like _____.

2- Canceled checks in the abandoned subway car seemed _____.

3- A spider under the rug is like _____.

4- Graffiti on the abandoned building like _____.

5- Nothing was the same, now that it was _____.

6- The dice rolled out of the cup toward Veronica like _____.

7- A child in _____ is like a _____ in _____.

8- _____ is like muscles stretched taut over bone.

9- The fog plumed through gunshot holes in the car windows like _____.

10- She held her life in her own hands as if it were _____.

11- Lacey poured coffee down her throat as if _____.

12- If I should wake before I die, _____.

13- The security guard walks the lobby as if _____.

14- The library books left in the rain like _____.

15- Music in the hallway like _____.

~*~

160

ABOUT THE AUTHOR

Josh Langston writes books which have amused, angered, enlightened and entertained many readers. He regularly mines history for background that's little known but reliably fascinating. His plots are complex, interconnected and layered with humor and suspense; his characters are rarely predictable, and even his bad guys tend to be both engaging and diabolical.

Langston's readers are rarely satisfied with just one of his books, whether it's part of a series or a stand-alone. He's proud to let his southern roots show in his characters and his choice of settings.

His two most recent novel releases are: **Treason, Treason!**, an alternate history/time travel adventure set in the American Revolution, and **A Primitive in Paradise**, book three in his series about Mato, the two-foot tall American Indian warrior.

When he's not working on a new novel, Langston is most likely editing, teaching, blogging, or helping his wonderful wife watch their amazing grandkids. He's even been known to goof off from time to time.

You can write to him at: **DruidJosh@gmail.com** or visit his blog at **www.JoshLangston.com**.

~*~

20056510R00098

Made in the USA
San Bernardino, CA
26 March 2015